ACCIDENTS

In North American Climbing 2017

Volume 11 | Number 2 | Issue 70

AMERICAN ALPINE CLUB
GOLDEN, COLORADO

ALPINE CLUB OF CANADA
CANMORE, ALBERTA

CONTENTS

Front Cover Photo: Rocky Mountain Rescue Group practicing high-angle rescue in Eldorado Canyon, Colorado. Photo by Alison Sheets. **Back Cover:** Photo by Andrew Bradberry.

© 2017 The American Alpine Club

ISBN: 978-1-933056-97-5; (e-book) 978-1-933056-99-9. Manufactured in the United States. Published by the American Alpine Club, 710 Tenth Street, Suite 100, Golden, CO, 80401, www.americanalpineclub.org.

WARNING!

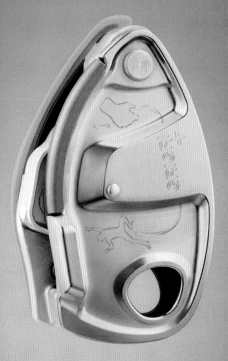

GRIGRI +
_____

The newest member of
the GRIGRI family.

ACCIDENTS IN NORTH AMERICAN CLIMBING

American Alpine Club

EDITOR EMERITUS
John E. (Jed) Williamson

EDITOR
Dougald MacDonald

ASSOCIATE EDITORS
Aram Attarian, R. Bryan Simon

CONTRIBUTING EDITORS
Joel Peach, Dave Weber

REGIONAL EDITORS
Andy Anderson (UT); Aram Attarian (Southeast);
Lindsay Auble & Lee Smith (CO); Marc Beverly
& Erin Weber (NM); Stacia Glenn (WA); Sarah
Koniewicz (Midwest); Molly Loomis (ID & WY);
Dara Miles (NY & PA); R. Bryan Simon (WV); Eric
Ratkowski (Shawangunks, NY); Rob McNitt &
Michael Wejchert (NH)

DESIGN
David Boersma

ADDITIONAL THANKS
Ron Funderburke, Ian Jackson, Jim Karn,
Liberty Mountain, Nathan Olsson, Leo Paik, Jim
Pasterczyk, Petzl, John Reilly, Michael Skaug,
Mark Stier, Christina Spohn, Rick Vance

Alpine Club of Canada

CHAIR, SAFETY COMMITTEE

Hai Pham
safety@alpineclubofcanada.ca

CANADIAN CONTENT EDITOR
Robert Chisnall
anam@alpineclubofcanada.ca

BEAL
JOKER

FEATURES
+ 9.1MM ROPE
+ WEIGHT: 53G/M
+ SINGLE, HALF, AND TWIN CERTIFIED
+ PERFORMANCE MINDED FOR
SPORT, TRAD, ALPINE, AND ICE CLIMBING

UIAA WATER REPELLENT®   GOLDEN DRY   DRY COVER

BEAL ATHLETE ANNE STRUBLE
ON KING RAILER 5.13B/C, THE HOOP, UINTAS, UTAH

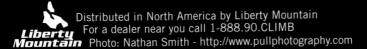

Distributed in North America by Liberty Mountain
For a dealer near you call 1-888.90.CLIMB
Photo: Nathan Smith - http://www.pullphotography.com

Liberty Mountain

PREFACE

By Dougald MacDonald

By late June, as we near the final stages of editing and designing this book, I start to feel a bit paranoid. I read and reread every report in *Accidents in North American Climbing* at least three times, and by the end, the accumulated weight of all these errors and lurking dangers makes me wonder if I'll ever be able to climb again. But of course I do, and each year I'm a little wiser.

I've been climbing for 40 years, and in the past five years, partly as a result of editing this book, I've learned more about safe climbing practices than ever before. The whole community seems more committed to safer climbing these days, including the American Alpine Club's broad new education program. In that spirit, I really do try to apply the lessons in these pages to my own climbing. I always recognize things I could do better.

One example is over-reliance on micro-cams. I love those little gizmos, but, as you'll see in this year's reports, they have real limitations for fall protection and anchors. I'm going to work harder at placing bomber pieces.

My second resolution is to more conscientiously test my rappel and lowering setups before I commit to them. I've never had an accident, but I've had several close calls when I realized I hadn't clipped into a rappel device properly or anchored securely when going off rappel. There's no excuse for botching these transitions, and I'm going to do better.

As you read through this year's edition, I hope you discover your own I-could-do better inspiration—the lessons that will make you a safer climber.

CONTRIBUTE

Submissions

Accidents in North American Climbing depends on detailed reports from injured climbers, their partners, search and rescue organizations, and park officials. Visit *publications.americanalpineclub.org/accidents_submission* to file a report online or email us at *accidents@americanalpineclub.org*.

Friends of Accidents

The following people and organizations have recently donated $100 or more specifically to support *Accidents*. Thank you! Make your own contribution at *americanalpineclub.org/donate*.

Jon Anderson
Charles Eiriksson Jr.
Carla Firey
Lee Freitag
James & Franziska Garrett
Eric Green
Michael Heathfield

Heidecorn Family Foundation
Stephen Johnson
Dougald MacDonald
Gary McElvany
William Oliver
Jon Pedder

Scott Petersen
Jim Small
Gary Treml
Jolene Unsoeld
Robert Wadja
Andrew Walker

THE SHARP END

Join the more than 15,000 people who listen to the Sharp End podcast each month. Hosted by Ashley Saupe, the Sharp End features interviews with climbers, rangers, and rescue professionals, based on the stories in *Accidents in North American Climbing*.

The Sharp End is sponsored for 2017 by Mammut, with additional support from Colorado Outward Bound School and Vertical Medicine Resources. Find it wherever you listen to podcasts.

AAC RESCUE BENEFITS

Members of the American Alpine Club are automatically enrolled for $12,500 of rescue benefits: $7,500 in Trailhead Rescue benefits (provided by Global Rescue), plus $5,000 in Domestic Rescue benefits to reimburse members for out-of-pocket rescue expenses within the United States.

Trailhead Rescue ($7,500)
This benefit covers you anywhere in the world for rescue by or under the direction of Global Rescue personnel. If you're injured beyond the trailhead, no matter the elevation, we will come to your aid. Members who want more than $7,500 of coverage can upgrade at a 5 percent discount by visiting americanalpineclub.org/rescue. TO USE THIS BENEFIT: Call +1 (617) 459-4200 as soon as possible during an emergency.

Domestic Rescue ($5,000)
This benefit reimburses AAC members for out-of-pocket rescue costs in the United States (Canada and Mexico excluded). This benefit can be used in addition to Trailhead Rescue. TO USE THIS BENEFIT: File a claim within 30 days of rescue by calling (303) 384-0110 or emailing claims@americanalpineclub.org.

Activities Covered
Climbing, hiking, backcountry skiing, mountain biking, and more. If it's human-powered, on land, and you're rescued, you're covered as long as you're an active AAC member. Note: Basic coverage does not include search, ambulance services, or medical care.

Upgrades
Planning to climb internationally? We recommend upgrading to a full Global Rescue membership with a 5 percent AAC discount. Upgrades include field rescue, medical consultation, and evacuation. Learn more: americanalpineclub.org/rescue.

BELAY ANCHORS

Beyond Acronyms: A Reasoned Approach to Anchor Building

BY RON FUNDERBURKE

Anchoring is a subject that is often debated and analyzed, and yet much of what is being proselytized or disparaged does not adhere to fundamental principles of physics, human factors psychology, or a working understanding of rock quality and material science. It is not entirely mysterious how American climbers have gotten to this point, but it is certainly mysterious that so many of us insist upon remaining in a scientific and practical abyss.

Anchoring has evolved. If we want to continue that evolution, it's valuable to explore the relationship between the past, the present, and the future. Today, anchoring is considered to be a precise, quantifiable art, but the science many climbers use to evaluate and quantify an anchor is dubious. Trusted and lauded concepts like *equalization* and *no extension* can be proven to be overvalued and/or inconsistently applied, which leaves us on uncertain footing.

If what we know about anchoring is questionable, what can we rely on? What does it mean when we say that anchors should be strong, secure, and simple?

HISTORY OF ANCHORING

The earliest written instructions for anchoring all emphasized the value of finding a reliable and unquestionable protection point. Rock horns, well-placed ironmongery, threaded holes and chockstones, and substantial vegetation all served to give a belayer enough security that his or her body belay would not be displaced by sudden dynamic loads. Importantly, climbers did not spend much time trying to quantify or calculate the properties of an anchor because the anchor was just one part of a system that depended largely on a gigantic human component: the belayer. Anchoring, as a skill set, was inextricable from the belay that relied on it.

Modern belay anchoring is much different. A belayer is not guarding the anchor with her own body weight or using the anchor simply to augment her stance. Instead, the anchor is expected to support a falling, resting, or lowering climber entirely, based on its own integrity and load-bearing capabilities. As a result, the anchor and its focal masterpoint have become the foundation

DIRECT BELAYS

Direct belays off the anchor are prudent when belaying a follower up to the anchor. They are advantageous because:

- The belayer's weight is not trapped in the system, eliminating the challenge of escaping the belay if the need arises.
- Direct belays can be quickly manipulated to haul or give assistance from above.
- It is easier to keep the rope tight if the follower is struggling.
- Direct belays do not put a counterweight load on the anchor or the components.

of most technical systems for climbing rock and ice. For example, when top-roping, the anchor is usually asked to hold the belayer and the climber in a counterweight arrangement. In direct belays, the anchor and its masterpoint are asked to sustain the weight of the seconding climber and any loads created to assist the seconding climber. In multi-pitch climbing, the anchor is asked to belay the second and then sustain the upward pull of the leader.

Whether we're top-roping or multi-pitch climbing, whether we're in the gym or at the crag, whether we're building anchors with bolts or trad gear, we are increasingly dependent completely on anchors. And building them has become a foundational skill in technical climbing.

ANCHORING PRINCIPLES AND ACRONYMS

A key aspect of modern anchors has been the development of acronyms used to teach and evaluate them. These acronyms are not without merit. They helped a generation of climbers inaugurate a new era in anchoring.

Anchor builders used such mnemonics like a checklist of key principles, and the anchors they created served climb after climb reliably and predictably. Here's how a typical anchoring scenario might unfold: The anchor builder, armed with a fundamental principle like SERENE, arrives at a pair of bolts. She begins to work through her acronym. She assesses the bolts and feels they are both strong. Knowing she'll need to build a redundant and equalized anchor, she selects a 7mm nylon cordelette as her attachment material. She doubles up the cord, clips one side to each bolt, targets the anticipated load, and then ties an overhand knot in such manner that creates two isolated legs and a masterpoint. She clips into the masterpoint with a locking carabiner and her clove-hitched climbing rope.

Before calling "off belay" she reviews her handiwork:
- Good bolts. 25 kN each, combining to 50kN at the masterpoint. Solid: Check.

ANCHORING ACRONYMS		
Acronym	Meaning	Ideal Context
SRENE	Solid, Redundant, Equalized, No Extension	Great for learning to build anchors on bolts with only one kind of material (e.g., 48-inch runner)
SERENE	Solid, Efficient, Redundant, Equalized, No Extension	Great for learning to build SRENE anchors when there are lots of options in the rigging materials
ERNEST	Equalized, Redundant, No Extension, Solid, Timely	Same as SERENE
EARNEST	Equalized, Angles, Redundant, No Extension, Solid, Timely	Ideal for anchors where the components might be farther apart
NERDSS	No Extension, Redundant, Distributes Load, Solid, Simple	Same as SRENE, plus great for understanding how load distribution can be manipulated
LEADSTER	Limit Extension, Angles, Direction, Solid, Timely, Equalized, Redundant	Same as SERENE

- One cordellette, one knot, 30 seconds to build. Efficient: Check.
- If any single part of this anchor up to the masterpoint were to fail, there are backups. Redundant: Check.
- When weighted, both legs of the anchor are tight. Equalized: Check.
- If anything were to break, the masterpoint wouldn't extend. No Extension: Check.

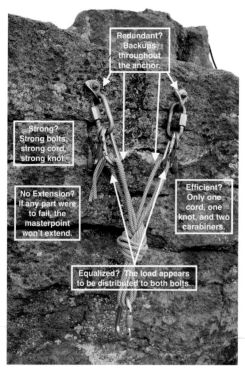

Redundant? Backups throughout the anchor.

Strong? Strong bolts, strong cord, strong knot.

No Extension? If any part were to fail, the masterpoint won't extend.

Efficient? Only one cord, one knot, and two carabiners.

Equalized? The load appears to be distributed to both bolts.

She's built a SERENE anchor. Millions of anchors have been constructed in approximately this fashion without incident or mishap, so it would be hasty to suggest that anchoring acronyms do not have value. However, climbers who also happen to be engineers, physicists, or just generally scientific-minded are quick to point out a fact that continues to elude a large number of climbers, climbing instructors, and authors of climbing books: Some of the qualities espoused in these beloved acronyms are not actually achieved in nature, neither practically, mathematically, nor experimentally.

Modern climbers have largely shifted from relying on the belayer's weight as a key part of the system to relying wholly on the qualities of an anchor, and yet many of the qualities we aspire to achieve are based on nuanced falsehoods. As anchoring situations grow more complex, a climber attempting to tick every box on such an anchor checklist can waste significant time trying to reach unattainable goals. Worse, the climber may be lulled into a false sense of security.

The time has come, as a climbing culture, that we confront the modern science to ensure that it aligns with modern anchors. That might mean that many of our beloved acronyms are best suited to teaching novices, instead of remaining our only checklist as we grow in the sport. But it also might allow our understanding to evolve as rapidly as our sport does.

THE MYTH OF EQUALIZATION

Anchors never really equalize. That is to say, they never manage to equally distribute the total load of the climbing team equally to all the components in the anchor, unless there is only one component. Yet, much false confidence and unnecessary time is contributed to achieving the elusive goal of equalization.

In experiment after experiment, the most carefully constructed anchor, with the most meticulous care taken to "equalize" all the components, will demonstrate that part of the anchor is holding most of the weight, most of the time. This is especially true if:

- The direction of the load alters in any way
- Any knots in the system tighten
- Any component fails
- The anchor builder intentionally ignores equalization in order to distribute more load to large components and less to small components (see photo at right)

As a result, anchors that funnel into a masterpoint do not succeed, as intended, in aggregating the strength of the things they are attached to. A *strong* anchor thus is only as strong as the component that is holding most of the weight most of the time.

With an appreciation for this reality, many climbers gravitate toward "self-equalizing" anchoring systems. Magic X and quad configurations have become popular, but their ability to self-adjust to variable load direction is not perfect. The climber imagines that the

[Top] Some anchors appear to be "equalized" when they actually distribute loads unequally. In this configuration, the 0.5 Camalot and the number 1 C3 are splitting roughly half the load while the number 2 Camalot takes the other half. The anchor builder recognized that one cam was the strongest piece and distributed the potential load with this in mind. [Bottom] As the load on a quad anchor setup changes direction, it appears that the components share the load throughout the range of motion. In fact, as the carabiner drags along the cord, peak loads can be transferred to a single piece while the anchor adjusts.

Even with limiting knots, failure of a component in a quad anchor system will create some extension.

shifting and sliding masterpoint allows equalization to happen, but in truth it only sort of happens...eventually...if the material doesn't create too much friction. In the meantime, as the masterpoint slides along, the bulk of the load spikes from one component to the next.

What's more, self-adjusting anchors all create opportunities for extension, despite the familiar anchoring acronyms' insistence upon *no extension*. Anchor builders are forced to qualify that rule, applying load-limiting knots that *limit* or *minimize* extension.

For years, we've been loyal to principles that are scientifically inaccurate, encourage us to miscalculate the strength of our anchor, and force us to make convenient exceptions to principles like "no extension." And while these acronyms enabled a generation of anchor builders to solve basic anchoring problems, in more complex scenarios these principles can easily become a liability.

WHY DO ANCHORS FAIL?

Indisputably, anchors fail because the load exceeds the force that the anchor can withstand. Theoretically, that should never happen because falling or lowering climbers create relatively small forces, given the capabilities of our equipment. So how does the load ever exceed the force an anchor can withstand? It happens in a few predictable and observable ways:

- *We use our equipment incorrectly.* It doesn't matter if the manufactured strength of a cam exceeds any load we could ever apply to it if we place the cam incorrectly. Similarly, a rope's strength is irrelevant if we tie knots incorrectly.
- *Our equipment has been damaged.* Chemicals or heat or trauma can cause imperceptible weaknesses in our equipment. We have to take good care of our gear.
- *The rock is not as good as we think it is.* Evaluation of rock, ice, vegetation, and other anchoring media is a critical skill, on a micro and macro level. If there are hidden weaknesses, an anchor will expose them.
- *We just make mistakes sometimes.* We can all appreciate that fatigue, haste, distraction, and peer pressure lead us to do uncharacteristic and dangerous things. It's part of being human.
- *Acts of nature happen.* There is such a thing as a no-win scenario in anchoring. We could do everything right and the mountain we're climbing could collapse around us. That's a bad day.

All this causality is actually good news. The list above is ordered according to factors that we have the most power and knowledge to prevent. We can learn to use our equipment correctly. We can take good care of our gear. We can evaluate the rock more carefully and more skeptically. We can learn to prevent most anchor failures by being careful and knowledgeable.

Such knowledge and care are part of what is keeping us safe out there, and if there are gaps in our knowledge, addressing the gap is vital. Instead of clinging to ideas like *equalization* and *no extension*, we can anticipate lurking dangers in our knowledge deficit.

FAILURE SCENARIOS
The following scenarios could be caused by a simplistic or inaccurate understanding of anchoring.

Small-component anchors. A devout loyalty to simple acronyms can have dangerous consequences when all the components in an anchor are smaller and weaker. If, for example, an anchor builder takes three small cams with 6kN of holding power each and imagines that an equalized masterpoint offers 18kN of combined strength, all the requirements of a SRENE anchor could be met. However, since equalization never really occurs, one of those pieces will be holding most of the weight most of the time. In that case, a single load that exceeds 6kN could sequentially rip every piece out of the rock. *Lesson Learned: Strive to build anchors in which at least one component is strong enough to hold any potential load the climbing team could create.*

Adjustable anchors. Anchors that self-adjust, like quad and sliding X configurations, do not eliminate extension. Mathematical data suggest the potential shock loads created by extension (even limited and minimized extensions) can be severe. If an anchor is constructed with only two pieces of equipment, like two 12kN cams, all the requirements of a SRENE anchor could be met. Yet a load large enough to make a single piece fail could catastrophically shock-load the second piece as well. *Lesson Learned: If you're using self-adjusting systems, make sure ALL*

[Top] "Equalizing" an anchor built from micr0-cams or other relatively weak components may create a false sense of security. [Middle] Self-adjusting anchors like the quad are still vulnerable to shock loads on the remaining pieces if one component fails. [Bottom] Combining two or more self-adjusting slings in an anchor allows the failure of one component to shock-load all the remaining pieces.

the components can survive the expected loads AND potential shock loads. Bomber pieces are required.

Stacked quads or Xs. Just as the self-adjusting properties of a single sliding X or quad configuration are imperfect, stacking these configurations multiplies those imperfections. The failure of a single piece proceeds to shock-load all the remaining pieces. *Lesson Learned: When stacking adjustable systems, make sure the components can handle expected loads AND potential shock loads.*

MORE COMPLEX ANCHORS

SERENE and EARNEST anchors are usually effective for simple top-rope anchors, but there are circumstances where an inability to escape that thinking could prove problematic. More complex anchors require more complex thinking and problem solving. These scenarios don't occur that often, but, as climbers' experience grows, most of us eventually will run into one or more of them:

- *The direction of load applied to an anchor changes.* The belayer could lean on an anchor in one direction, the belay might tug the anchor in a different direction, and two climbers at an anchor might fidget and tug and lean in lots of directions. Belay transitions on multi-pitch climbs can offer dramatic direction of load changes too. Typically, the anchor is rigged to belay a second climber, and then the same anchor is used for the lead belayer. The two loads could be completely different.

- *The components available for anchoring might be vastly dissimilar.* Some cams are rated to hold over 14kN, while the smallest cams may be rated to hold less than 6kN. Even if equalization were achievable in an anchor, why would anyone expect these two cams to do equal work? They are not equally valuable components. When anchoring components have vastly dissimilar

The anchor builder here has placed smaller components as backups for the bolt, but doesn't want the primary load distributed to them. The double length of material on the bolt and the single length of material on the small pieces (linked with clove hitches) achieves the desired result.

load-bearing properties, the rigging will have to be more complicated.
- A *climber often has to construct an anchor with limited resources.* The values and principles of anchoring do not change, but building a fundamentally sound anchor with limited resources is very challenging. It often requires some innovative and artistic problem-solving, hence the complexity.

The situations described above might coincide and overlap. Moreover, there is such a thing as a no-win scenario in climbing, when the available resources, the working skill set, or other circumstances will not allow an appropriate anchor for a direct belay to be built. In such cases, belayers might choose to insert their own bodies into the system, finding a solid stance, belaying off the harness, and relying on the anchor as a backup only. In extreme cases, a tactical retreat or a call for assistance is preferable to settling for an anchor that may well result in catastrophic failure.

THE TRIPLE S: FUNDAMENTALS OF COMPLEX ANCHORS

When anchoring becomes more complicated, a more sophisticated approach positions the anchor builder to answer three basic questions:

Is the anchor **strong** enough?
Is the anchor **secure** enough?
Is the anchor as **simple** as it can be?

This is a broader, more inclusive way to think about anchors than the SERENE-style mnemonic. Call it the Triple S approach. Triple S anchors do not strive to equalize or to eliminate extensions; they strive to distribute load intelligently, minimize extensions, and avoid edge-case failure scenarios. Triple S anchors do not attempt to aggregate strength; they rely on unquestionably strong component parts and anticipate a human factor in that calculation. Triple S anchors do not muddle into unnecessary complexity; they solve the anchoring problem as efficiently as possible.

Strength. An anchor must be adequately strong to sustain all potential loads applied to it. Then, an anchor's strength must be padded with a margin of error that could account for any number of mistakes that all humans are wont to make. Let's be conservative and provide ourselves with a 100 percent margin of error. That would mean that any anchor should be strong enough to sustain all potential loads applied to it multiplied by two.

Security. This means that if anything unexpected happens—components fail, the direction of load changes—the anchor must survive those unexpected changes. An anchor that is secure has backups. It has systemic redundancy all the way to the masterpoint. If any single point in the anchor were to fail, other points would provide adequate backups. We make a few exceptions for anchors that are so titanic in nature (large, stable trees and boulders) that we might rely upon these single features alone, but even these features could be rigged in a redundant fashion.

Simplicity. A climber needs to appreciate that any anchor can quickly become convoluted and overly complex if it is rigged to solve phantom hazards or improbable

[Left] The anchor builder has constructed a SERENE anchor, but no single component is strong enough to hold all potential loads. Secure and Simple, but not Strong. [Middle] Appreciating that the components are relatively weak, the anchor builder deploys an "equalette" configuration, in an attempt at load sharing. But this configuration requires more knots and more time, and still has shock-loading potential. It's likely Stronger than the first anchor, but not Simple. [Right] The third anchor adds a well-placed number 1 Camalot, doubles the amount of material in that leg, incorporates the smaller pieces as backups, and only needs three knots to tie the whole rig. Strong, Simple, and Secure.

contingencies, or if it slavishly adheres to anchoring principles that are unachievable. For any given anchor, simplicity refers to the overall amount of time to construct and deconstruct an anchor. Simplicity refers to the amount of equipment needed, including rope, slings, carabiners, and any amount of padding or edge protection. All this should be minimized. Simplicity also refers to the number of knots being tied and untied, the number of steps needed to construct the anchor, and the distance the components are separated. All these should be minimized too.

When time, equipment, and number of steps are all minimized, and an anchor still demonstrates adequate strength and security, an anchor will have achieved the best end result our current knowledge and technology can offer.

LEARNING ANCHOR CRAFT

Significant portions of American climbers enjoy contexts where anchor-building skills are largely irrelevant. Most bouldering requires no form of technical hardware. Most indoor climbing involves pre-established anchors that participants can learn to use quickly. Most sport climbing involves anchor bolts where a pair of quickdraws can quickly suffice.

However, it's important to acknowledge the necessity of the anchoring skill set that arrives with each new context. As soon as climbers leave the gym and venture out to their local top-roping crag, for example, the available anchors might be widely variable. Some crags, like Pilot Mountain in North Carolina, offer an abundance of bolts for anchoring top-ropes, but staying safe at the cliff's edge will require a completely separate skill set. Another crag, like Devil's Lake in Wisconsin or Great Falls in Virginia, will not have any of those hardware options. Top-roping teams will need diverse anchor-building skills, the knowledge to assess natural components like boulders and trees, the skill to place solid removable protection, and the ability to access a cliff's edge safely. Even though crags like these are of modest stature, the anchor setups are not trivial, and climbers will quickly find themselves dealing with the kinds of scenarios that make anchor building more complicated. Of course, when it comes to mountaineering, traditional multi-pitch climbing, or ice climbing, creative and thoughtful anchoring skills are an integral and unavoidable part of the security of the team.

So, a climber that may not have learned to anchor through indoor pursuits, bouldering, or sport climbing might legitimately ask: If I need to anchor to pursue other genres of the sport, how do I learn?

Step 1: Study
All the information that anyone needs to know about anchoring is available in scores of books and articles. Appreciate that anchoring is an art and a craft, and all great artists and craftsmen study the work of the masters.

Step 2: Become an Anchor Analyst
Climbing with a skilled mentor can provide many working examples of the craft. When you analyze anchors, try to appreciate that there are dozens of ways to build fundamentally sound anchors. Every one you encounter provides an opportunity to dissect the skills and decision-making that were used to create them.

Step 3: Ground School
Head out to a boulder field or the base of a crag and build anchors. Analyze the anchors you build. Take a photo of your anchor, send it to a friend or an instructor, and ask for feedback. It's best to make these experiments (and mistakes) in a risk-neutral setting.

Step 4: Take a Class or Hire a Guide
Formal instruction from a good climbing instructor or a guide with a knack for teaching can be the most efficient way to find out what you don't know. A professional can see the patterns in your skill set that you can't see because you are still learning. The cost of a class or a guide may seem onerous, but it's most effective to pinpoint bad habits and gaps in reasoning early on, before those skills become engrained. That is worth a premium for any climber.

Step 5: Ease into Real Anchoring
Select climbs that have straightforward anchoring challenges *and* moderate climbing difficulties. Look for lines that follow a continuous crack system. Avoid climbs that have traverses, roofs, or downclimbs off the belay. These climbs will all require anchors that adjust to wildly variable load directions.

The more you get into anchor building, the more you seek feedback and advice from others, the more of an analyst you become, the more you will learn and the more terrain and climbs you will be able to experience. However, if the history of anchoring teaches us anything, it teaches us that new technologies and new horizons will always challenge what we think we know. That won't be problem unless we start to trick ourselves into thinking we already know everything.

Ron Funderburke is education director of the American Alpine Club. A more comprehensive version of this article, with additional photos and examples, can be found in the Know the Ropes Index section at www.americanalpineclub.org.

The West Ridge (left) and Redgarden Wall of Eldorado Canyon State Park. *Craig Hoffman*

Danger Zones

ELDORADO CANYON

BY JOEL PEACH

Even at a distance, the sound of a person hitting the ground after a 70-foot fall is unmistakable. On April 9, 2016, I was approaching the Whale's Tail in Eldorado Canyon to follow a novice trad climber up his first lead in the Colorado state park. Hearing a commotion, we rushed over to the base of Redgarden Wall to see if we could help. A climber lay badly broken on the trail, rope still attached to his harness, while another climber held his head and we both assessed his injuries. A fun day out had gone horribly wrong.

Paramedics arrived to stabilize the climber. Rocky Mountain Rescue Group packaged and evacuated him to a nearby road, where an ambulance waited. A helicopter soon delivered him to a level-one trauma center. As our adrenaline receded and the climber's long road to recovery began, so did my own journey to understand why such accidents happen in Eldorado Canyon and what might be done to prevent more of them, both here and at similar multi-pitch traditional climbing areas around North America.

"Eldo" is home to ruddy sandstone formations up to about 800 feet high, hosting well over 1,000 rock routes. Approximately 95 percent of the routes require climbers to place and remove their own protection (the rest are top-ropes or bolted climbs); a majority of climbs do not have fixed anchors at belay stations; and there are hundreds of multi-pitch routes and link-ups. Eldo's complex cliffs present extra challenges to climbers, including route-finding, occasional loose rock, inconsistent protection opportunities, and complicated and exposed descent routes. Nevertheless, in key respects, the accidents that occur here—and the lessons derived from them—are similar to those in other traditional climbing areas, from North Conway to Devils Tower, and from desert sandstone to Squamish granite.

To better understand Eldorado Canyon's accident history, I analyzed 75 incident reports published in the last 30 years of *Accidents in North American Climbing*. In addition, the *Accidents* editors met with rangers at Eldorado Canyon State Park and reviewed data prepared by rangers and by Rocky Mountain Rescue Group, the main search and rescue organization serving the park. Here, we present the most common causes of climber accidents and rescues in Eldorado, along with recommendations to prevent or mitigate them.

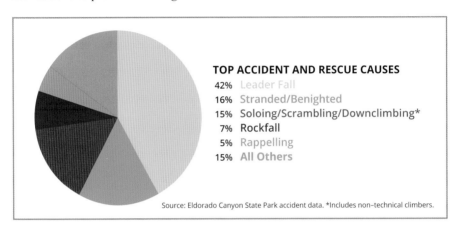

TOP ACCIDENT AND RESCUE CAUSES

42% Leader Fall
16% Stranded/Benighted
15% Soloing/Scrambling/Downclimbing*
7% Rockfall
5% Rappelling
15% All Others

Source: Eldorado Canyon State Park accident data. *Includes non-technical climbers.

FALLS

By a large margin, falling while climbing is the most likely way to end up in the pages of *Accidents*, and Eldorado Canyon is no exception. Over half of all the incidents documented in the various Eldo studies involved falls—most of them leader falls.

In many of these cases, one or more pieces of protection pulled out during the fall, causing the leader to plunge farther than expected and suffer an injury. Often the piece that pulled was the first and only one on a pitch, leading to a ground or ledge fall. As the Eldorado rangers recommend at the state park's website, "Never have only one piece of protection between you and a catastrophic fall." Sometimes multiple pieces failed. The climber I encountered last April below Redgarden Wall had pulled out his top two pieces (both micro-cams) in a fall, causing him to plummet all the way to the ground on the sparsely protected climb (see page 56.)

Unlike the continuous, splitter crack systems found in many trad areas, Eldorado's cracks tend to form irregularly and intermittently. Although the hard sandstone lends itself to solid protection with both nuts and cams, the leader will encounter a wide variety of placement types, including cracks, flakes, undercuts, and pockets. As a result, more skill and practice with gear placements are required. A look through the Eldorado guidebook or websites will reveal many climbs with PG-13 or R ratings, indicating difficult protection or serious run-outs. The newcomer to Eldo would be wise to start with better-protected G- or PG-rated climbs.

Many Eldo routes climb past ledges, big and small, that present significant hazards in long falls. Care must be taken to protect early and frequently above these features to minimize the possibility of contacting a ledge. Fixed protection, including rusty pitons dating back to the 1950s or '60s, should be backed up with a solid nut or cam whenever possible.

Like any crag, Eldorado has had its share of belay errors. These generally are not specific to traditional climbing, but certain issues may be raised by multi-pitch climbs. In 2015, for example, a climber following the second pitch of the Naked Edge (5.11) asked the leader to lower him a few feet after retrieving a stuck piece; the leader was belaying directly off the anchor in autoblock mode, and he accidentally caused the belay device to release the second's weight, leading to a long fall.

In at least two documented instances, leaders strayed off-route onto more difficult and run-out terrain before falling. Some of Eldorado's cliffs can present a maze of shallow corners and indistinct features, making close study of the guidebook and other resources essential. There also have been several reported cases of leaders failing to protect routes adequately for their seconds, causing them to take swinging and damaging falls. In one instance, the second climber on a traversing route cleaned all of the leader's protection, leaving the third climber up the route vulnerable to a pendulum fall that ended with a broken leg.

Our review also included a number of unroped falls. Free soloing, unroped downclimbing, and scrambling add up to one of the largest causes of accidents in Eldorado Canyon State Park's data. (Some of these victims were non-technical climbers who scrambled up the park's easy-to-access cliffs.) It's generally not possible to say what might have caused these climbers to fall, but many popular Eldorado climbs require the use of suspect flakes or chockstones as holds, and these eventually come loose. Less dire but still a significant contributor to Eldorado injuries are bouldering falls. In the state park's recent accident data, bouldering is listed among the top five accident types.

TOP 6 INCIDENT SITES

1. Bastille Crack, Bastille
2. East Slabs Descent, Redgarden Wall
3. Calypso and variations, Wind Tower
4. Rewritten, Redgarden Wall
5. Werk Supp, Bastille
6. Yellow Spur, Redgarden Wall*

Source: Eldorado Canyon State Park data. *Rewritten, Werk Supp, and Yellow Spur each had the same number of incidents.

LOOSE ROCK

Although the good rock in Eldorado Canyon is firm, compact sandstone, many routes also pass through areas of loose or suspect rock. Eldo's location in the foothills of the Rocky Mountains sees large seasonal temperature swings, freezing cycles, and occasional severe rain and hailstorms. These weather patterns combine to create increased risk from falling rock, especially after a recent storm.

Rocks often collect on ledges where they can be knocked off by climbers or storms. Some descent routes (notably along the West Ridge and the west side of Redgarden Wall) traverse ledges directly above popular climbs; rappel routes may lie above areas where climbers congregate. Many Eldo climbing routes pass directly through (or have belay stances on) various "rotten bands" of darker, highly fractured, and sharp sandstone. Great care is required in these areas or wherever loose rock congregates. Leaders should test holds and flakes before pulling on them or placing gear behind them, and any climber should yell "ROCK!" loudly and repeatedly if something falls.

The falling rocks in our reports ranged from a few inches to "person size" and larger. (In 2002, a rock estimated to be 3x4x6 feet fell from the Bastille and exploded onto the road below, fortunately without hitting anyone.) Two incidents involved climbers walking at the base of cliffs. In one case, a broken hold struck the leader in the abdomen (causing a fall) and then continued downward to hit the belayer in the legs, forcing a rescue and helicopter evacuation. In 2002, a climber was traversing a rotten band on the fourth pitch of the popular Yellow Spur when he pulled off a loose rock that fell onto a finger and nearly severed it.

Leader falls are by far the most common cause of climber injuries in Eldorado Canyon. *Craig Hoffman*

An analysis of incidents from 1998–2011 published by Rocky Mountain Rescue Group showed rockfall incidents in Eldo reaching their highest levels in spring and early summer, suggesting a correlation with the post-winter thaw. In our *Accidents* data, we saw concentrations of rockfall incidents in early summer but also in the fall and in February—it's a year-round threat.

Natural and spontaneous rockfall is not uncommon in Eldorado Canyon (including occasional very large and destructive landslides); however, all but one of the rockfall reports in our records indicated that other climbers were confirmed or suspected to be overhead. People should avoid climbing or rappelling below other parties. Consider avoiding areas known for rockfall hazard (such as the Rewritten/Great Zot area of Redgarden or the upper West Ridge) on weekends.

Perhaps most obviously, wear a helmet. While a helmet is no match for a television-size block, it certainly can prevent or minimize injury from smaller debris. Note that many people only don their helmets once they begin climbing. The prudent Eldorado climber will wear one while belaying, hanging out below busy crags, or while hiking climbers' trails below the cliffs.

STRANDING AND BENIGHTING

In our reports and in Eldorado Canyon's data, getting stuck on or atop a climb is one of the most common incidents reported, frequently requiring rescues. All of this book's reports of stranding (save one for which there was no route data) took place on Redgarden Wall, which has the park's longest and most complex routes (up to 8 or 9 pitches) and descents. Some Redgarden routes top out along a good descent trail. But others require hard-to-follow rappel lines or a long, exposed descent along the East Slabs, where fourth-class terrain and an inobvious route make it easy to get stalled out the first time you do it. Rocky Mountain Rescue Group also has been called out to rescue several climbers stuck on Shirt Tail Peak, the highest summit in the park.

Half of the climbers who needed help descending were caught out after dark, many without headlamps. One stranding involved the inability of the party to hear each other. (Wind and the roar from South Boulder Creek can make communication difficult between leader and followers.) The belayer tied off his climber and went to get help; eventually, a rescue team was able to rappel to the stuck climber and help him descend.

Fortunately, despite the frequent need for rescue, no injuries were reported among the stranding incidents. In one case, a party was able to self-rescue but not before spending a chilly March night out in T-shirts; they concluded, "It was a pretty miserable experience."

The main strategy to avoid stranding is adequate preparation. Climbers should thoroughly research descent routes from the major cliffs, carry a description copied from the guidebook or online sources, and familiarize themselves with backup descents in case plans change during the day. An early start on long routes is crucial to allow time to complete an unfamiliar climb or descent. Always toss a headlamp in the pack or clip one to the back of your harness as an additional measure of insurance.

LOWERING AND RAPPELLING

A crop of incidents in recent years—all involving injury or fatality—indicate that climbers are making costly mistakes when lowering their partners in Eldorado. In four incidents reported in *Accidents*, the end of the climbing rope slipped through the belay device because the rope was not long enough to return the lowering climber to the ground. In two others, there was a miscommunication and a leader fell after leaning back from an anchor, thinking he or she would be lowered.

Such incidents are hardly unique to Eldorado Canyon or to traditional climbing areas—indeed they have become increasingly common in the sport climbing and gym era. It's possible that some newcomers to Eldorado have an expectation that anchors will be set at heights convenient for lowering with a single rope. In fact, however, most Eldorado anchors are set irrespective of their height above the ground, using available trees or ledges. In other words, these were never intended to be lowering anchors.

As a result, climbers must study the guidebook or obtain other beta to ensure their rope length is adequate to lower a leader. In certain cases, a two-rope rappel will be the only way to descend from a single-pitch climb. Other anchors may allow lowering, but only to a ledge above the ground, from which downclimbing will be required. As a precaution, belayers should always close the system by tying in to their end of the rope or knotting the free end, either of which will prevent the rope from being fed through the belay device while lowering.

As with lowering, the types of rappelling accidents seen in Eldorado Canyon are not unique to the area. Reports show two main causes: anchor failure and rappelling off the end of the rope. In one of the anchor failures, climbers were practicing rappels when a sling appears to have disconnected from a locking carabiner. In another case, a single-point anchor failed when the second climber leaned back to rappel. In several cases, climbers rappelled off the ends of their ropes.

Many rappelling and lowering accidents are caused by misjudging the length of rope required. *Craig Hoffman*

Climbers should study route descriptions to ensure they have adequate length ropes (or if two ropes are needed) for rappels. Anchors should be checked carefully. Although many rappel anchors in Eldorado now are equipped with modern bolts, many others rely on slings around trees or blocks. Don't hesitate to replace faded or damaged slings; make sure trees are at least five inches thick, well-rooted, and healthy; test blocks or chockstones to ensure they are solid. Backing up rappels with a "third hand" (friction hitch) and tying knots in the end of the rope should be standard procedure on any Eldo rappel.

DEGREE OF DIFFICULTY

Eldorado Canyon has many excellent climbs in the lower to middle grades, and unsurprisingly these are both very popular and also the scene of many accidents. When the state park looked at its accident records, it found that about two-thirds of Eldorado's climbing accidents involved routes 5.8 or easier.

That said, our review of reports in *Accidents in North American Climbing* shows a distribution of incidents throughout Eldo's range of difficulty. (With one exception, the Eldorado reports in this year's edition involve climbs rated 5.10 or harder.) Though conventional wisdom suggests that Eldo's sandbagged "moderates" pick off a disproportionate number of novices, it's clear that the ability to climb harder grades will not protect you.

The best advice for safer climbing in Eldo holds true for many similar areas: Arrive equipped with appropriate gear and prepared with solid fundamentals for placing protection, belaying, and rappelling. For climbs involving more than one pitch, study the route up and the way down, and make a plan to retreat if necessary. Be realistic about your abilities and flexible in response to conditions, and you'll enjoy one of the nation's highest concentrations of quality traditional climbs.

Joel Peach is a contributing editor of this publication. Thanks to Steve Muehl-hauser, Mike McHugh, Alison Sheets, and Rocky Mountain Rescue Group for their help with this article. Previous "Danger Zones" articles have analyzed the accident histories of Mt. Rainier, the Nose of El Capitan, and the Exum Ridge on the Grand Teton. All are available at publications.americanalpineclub.org.

Red circle marks the location of a climber stranded on Mt. Hunter's west ridge by high avalanche danger during an attempted winter ascent. *Dave Weber*

ALASKA

STRANDED BY AVALANCHE DANGER
Mt. Hunter, West Ridge

A climber departed Talkeetna on January 21 for a planned 65-day winter solo expedition on the west ridge of Mt. Hunter. At 7 a.m. on April 1, the Alaska Region Communication Center (ARCC) received an emergency notification and GPS coordinates from the climber's SPOT device. At 10 a.m. the state's Rescue Coordination Center deployed two aircraft from Alaska Air National Guard to the GPS location of the SPOT notification. A fixed-wing aircraft was able to establish radio communication with the climber from above a thick cloud layer. The climber said he was at approximately 8,600 feet on the west ridge and was not injured but was low on food and fuel. He was unable to ascend or descend due to avalanche conditions, and he requested evacuation.

Weather prevented further rescue efforts for the remainder of April 1 and all of April 2. By this time, NPS mountaineering rangers Chris Erickson and Dave Weber and the park's contract H125 helicopter both had returned to Talkeetna from work elsewhere and were able to assume control of the mission. At noon on April 3, pilot Andreas Hermansky and rangers Erickson and Weber executed a successful short-haul evacuation of the climber via rescue basket and returned him to Talkeetna.

ANALYSIS

This climber was well prepared and traveled judiciously throughout his lengthy expedition. Even with ample arctic solo-expedition experience and sound logistical decision-making during his trip, the climber was stranded for nearly a week by a storm delivering high snowfall. As his supplies neared exhaustion at his camp on the ridge, he made, as he described it, "the horribly difficult decision" to call for a rescue. To his credit, this climber had contemplated myriad potential solutions and attempted numerous retreats before determining that he could not extract himself safely without assistance. (*Source: Denali Mountaineering Rangers.*)

SEVERE HIGH ALTITUDE ILLNESS
Denali, West Buttress

On April 17 the "Gonna Die!" expedition team flew to the Kahiltna Glacier for a planned 21-day ascent of the West Buttress climbing route. Expedition Gonna Die! was the first team of the 2016 season to reach the 14,200-foot camp and the only expedition camped in the basin at the time of this incident.

At 11:45 a.m. on April 24, eight days after flying onto the glacier, the team contacted the Alaska Region Communication Center (ARCC) by satellite phone. The team's text message requested immediate evacuation of a climber from 14,200 feet. The 26-year-old male was suffering from suspected high altitude pulmonary edema (HAPE) and high altitude cerebral edema (HACE). The patient had a persistent uncontrollable cough, audible fluid in the lungs, a headache, and showed signs of ataxia (loss of muscle coordination).

ARCC contacted the mountaineering rangers in Talkeetna, and at 1:17 p.m. the NPS contract H125 helicopter, piloted by Andreas Hermansky, departed Talkeetna with mountaineering ranger Joey McBrayer aboard. The climber was evacuated from the 14,200-foot camp and assessed and treated for HAPE and HACE by McBrayer en route to Talkeetna. The patient was then transferred to a local hospital via ambulance for further monitoring. The remaining two members of expedition descended from 14,200 feet to base camp without incident.

ANALYSIS
This case highlights the need for early recognition and descent when severe altitude illness presents. Both HAPE and HACE can quickly incapacitate a climber and make self-evacuation impossible. Early symptoms that should raise suspicion include excessive fatigue for HAPE and unresolved, worsening acute mountain sickness for HACE. In both cases, descent until the symptoms resolve is appropriate. (*Source: Denali Mountaineering Rangers.*)

FROSTBITE AT HIGH CAMP
Denali, West Buttress

At 11:17 a.m. on May 25, a 49-year-old male and his 40-year-old male climbing partner contacted the mountaineering rangers at 14,200 feet via family radio service (FRS) to report that both individuals had deep frostbite injuries. The injured climbers were camped at 17,200 feet on Denali's West Buttress Route. They reported that the injuries had been sustained during their ascent from 14,200-foot camp to high camp the day before.

The 49-year-old climber reported deep frostbite in both of his hands, and the 40-year-old reported deep frostbite in both of his feet. The climbers requested a rescue due to their inability to safely navigate the technical terrain below the 17,200-foot camp with their injuries. At the time of the initial radio communication, the team said they were prepared to remain in camp "for several days" as a significant storm event enveloped the mountain and prevented safe travel between the two camps.

During the storm, the climbers and mountaineering rangers maintained regular radio contact to discuss treatment recommendations and evacuation plans. When the storm subsided on May 28, three days after the initial report, the patients and NPS personnel rendezvoused at 15,400 feet on the West Buttress. Following a thorough assessment of both climbers, the patient with frostbitten hands was assisted on foot to 14,200-foot camp, while the patient with frostbitten feet was packaged and transported via ski toboggan to prevent further injury. The patients remained under NPS care overnight and then evacuated to Talkeetna by helicopter on May 29. A frostbite specialist subsequently evaluated both climbers at a hospital in Wasilla, Alaska.

ANALYSIS

Frostbite injuries can have debilitating and long-lasting consequences. It is of paramount importance to actively rewarm any body parts that become numb while climbing in cold conditions, by windmilling the arms to move blood to the fingers, for example, or by placing the affected extremities on your own or a partner's warm, bare skin. If unable to rewarm a cooling body part, climbers must seek shelter or descend to more hospitable conditions to prevent further frostbite injury.

If stranded by conditions, as these climbers were, frozen tissue should be rewarmed by skin-to-skin contact or a warm-water bath (99–102°F/37–39°C), but only if there is no chance of refreezing the tissue. Do not rub the affected areas. (*Source: Denali Mountaineering Rangers.*)

ANOTHER FROSTBITE CASE REQUIRING EVACUATION: *On June 6, a 62-year-old climber was evacuated via helicopter from 14,200-foot camp due to severe frostbite injuries to the fingers and toes of all four extremities, preventing his safe descent to base camp under his own power.*

HIGH ALTITUDE CEREBRAL EDEMA
Denali, West Buttress

The four climbers of expedition "TEAM ECS'16" flew to Kahiltna base camp at 7,200 feet on May 31. Thirteen days later, on June 12, TEAM ECS'16 moved to 17,200-foot camp and then left for a summit attempt the following day. Throughout the day, this team interacted with expedition "Mountain Wolverun" at multiple points along the climbing route. At 11 p.m., TEAM ECS'16 was descending from the summit as Mountain Wolverun was ascending the final ridge. The two teams met again at 19,500 feet at 1:30 a.m. During this encounter, members of expedition Mountain Wolverun noted that one member of TEAM ECS'16, a 66-year-old man, appeared to exhausted and having some difficulty walking—signs and symptoms of possible high altitude cerebral edema (HACE).

One member of Mountain Wolverun remained with TEAM ECS'16 while his two teammates continued their descent to 17,200-foot camp. Those on scene reported that the sick climber quickly deteriorated, and at 18,500 feet, near Zebra Rocks, his eyesight failed. Subsequent to this development, the patient became disoriented and was no longer able to walk. The climber from Mountain Wolverun determined that a ground rescue with the limited number of climbers present was not feasible, and he descended solo to request help from mountaineering rangers.

At 5:25 a.m. the Alaska Region Communication Center (ARCC) received an emergency call from the solo climber via satellite phone. The mountaineering ranger on call received notification at 5:35 a.m. and began to mobilize rescue resources. At 7:30 a.m., Andreas Hermansky piloted the NPS contract helicopter from Talkeetna to 14,200-foot camp to retrieve mountaineering ranger Dan Corn for a reconnaissance flight. It was determined that a short-haul operation utilizing a rescue basket would be the best method, given the patient's location and altitude.

Monitoring a Portable Altitude Chamber in the medical tent at the 14,200-foot camp on Denali's West Buttress Route. *Menno Boermans*

At approximately 8:50 a.m., the patient was loaded into the rescue basket attached to the end of the rescue line and flown down to 14,200-foot camp, where advanced medical interventions were initiated. At 9:46 a.m., advanced life support was discontinued and the patient was pronounced deceased.

ANALYSIS

Climbers must remain diligent in assessing themselves and their teammates for symptoms of high altitude illness. If altitude illness presents, teams should descend immediately to an elevation where the patient returns to his or her normal baseline. It is unclear when this patient first began to experience symptoms of HACE, but, typically, by the time a patient presents with ataxia (difficulty walking) it is too late for self-evacuation.

In the high alpine arctic environment, ground rescue can be extremely physically taxing. The difficulty for rescuers is amplified when a patient becomes non-ambulatory. Climbers in such situations face a predicament in deciding whether to remain on scene to assist a companion or leave to summon additional resources. A radio or other communication device may help, but even then the decision-making may be difficult. Attempting to provide the greatest good for the greatest number of people, including the patient, his or her companions, and the rescuers, should be the guiding principle. (*Source: Denali Mountaineering Rangers.*)

HACE REQUIRING EVACUATION: *On June 26, a climber at 14,200-foot camp on the West Buttress Route began exhibiting the symptoms of HACE. Her team had followed an average ascent profile, traveling nine days from 7,200-foot camp to reach 14,200 feet. The patient initially complained of a severe headache (10/10 on pain scale) and blurred vision. When she failed to respond to medications provided by her guide, she was transported to the NPS medical tent for additional care, including oxygen therapy and hyperbaric chamber treatments, and was evacuated to Talkeetna by helicopter on June 27.*

HIGH ALTITUDE PULMONARY EDEMA
Denali, West Buttress

On June 16, a mountain guide radioed NPS mountaineering rangers from the upper West Buttress Route to say that one of his clients was exhibiting signs and symptoms of high altitude pulmonary edema (HAPE). The guided group was returning from a summit attempt when the patient began to experience significant respiratory distress. The guide had begun an appropriate medication regime for HAPE and continued descent toward high camp. Mountaineering rangers responded from the 17,200-foot camp toward Denali Pass to rendezvous with the descending group. Ranger Mik Shain and his rescue patrol volunteers assisted the patient back to his tent in camp after midnight for further assessment and treatment. Once in camp, the patient began receiving supplemental oxygen via nasal cannula, starting at 2:39 a.m., yet still deteriorated over the following hours.

Based on the patient's status, rangers Joey McBrayer, Tucker Chenoweth, and Joe Reichert initiated plans for a rescue attempt at first light. Pilot Andreas Hermansky departed Talkeetna at 4:15 a.m. in the H125 helicopter and retrieved ranger Dave Weber from 7,200-foot camp. After the patient was loaded into the helicopter at high camp, Weber assessed the patient in flight and, with minimal improvement observed during a nearly 17,000-foot descent, he requested air medical transport to definitive medical care. In Talkeetna the patient was transferred to Alaska LifeMed and flown to a local hospital.

ANALYSIS
Shortness of breath at rest is one of the hallmark signs of HAPE. Excessive fatigue can be a precursor to the onset of clinical HAPE, warning of pending patient deterioration. Such fatigue should be considered as justification to forgo a planned ascent before this form of altitude illness becomes an emergency. (*Source: Denali Mountaineering Rangers.*)

FALL WHILE DOWNCLIMBING | Failure to Self-Arrest
Denali, West Buttress

On June 13, the six members of expedition "Extreme Travel" completed their orientation at the Talkeetna ranger station and flew to the Kahiltna Glacier to begin a West Buttress climb. The team moved to 17,200-foot camp on the eighth day of their trip. Despite a more rapid ascent profile than normally recommended, all members of the group reported feeling well.

On June 22, four members of the expedition departed for the summit. During their descent in the early morning hours of June 23, one of the climbers lost his footing and fell in the area of Zebra Rocks, at nearly 18,400 feet. This fall pulled the entire rope team off their feet, and none of the climbers was able to self-arrest on the hard snow surface. One climber sustained a closed head injury and was unresponsive for approximately 10 minutes, while another climber sustained a chest wall injury and possible broken rib(s).

The two uninjured teammates descended to high camp in search of assistance. They reached camp between 3 a.m. and 4 a.m. and made contact with Alaska Mountaineering School lead guide Rob Gowler, who relayed accident and patient status information to the NPS mountaineering rangers via radio. Based upon the severity of injuries reported, incident command decided that a helicopter rescue attempt would be most prudent. Pilot Andreas Hermansky flew to 14,200-foot camp, where mountaineering ranger Coley Gentzel boarded for a reconnaissance flight. A lenticular cloud over the mountain had descended to the area where the injured climbers were located and prevented a rescue

Moderately steep snow climbing in the Zebra Rocks area, above 18,000 feet on Denali's West Buttress Route. *Dave Weber*

attempt at that time. Hermansky returned to 7,200-foot camp to await an improvement in weather conditions near Denali Pass.

Meanwhile, that morning, multiple teams had departed 17,200-foot camp, headed toward the summit. At 8:25 a.m., Alpine Ascents International mountain guide Erin Pollock reached the location of the injured party. Pollock reported that both the climber with the injured rib(s) and the climber with the suspected head injury were ambulatory, and that, given these changes, the team felt they could descend to high camp with assistance from climbers on the route. Over the next hour, several other teams arrived at Denali Pass and a plan was devised to help the climbers back to camp. Blaine Horner of the "Compass Data" expedition (a former volunteer with the NPS mountaineering rangers) abandoned his own summit attempt to assist the two men. Horner safely managed a nearly four-hour descent of the headwall to high camp, where they arrived at 1:10 p.m. The injured climbers eventually descended the mountain under their own power.

ANALYSIS

This incident highlights an important principle regarding roped team travel. When snow surface conditions are soft and conducive to self-arresting, it may be appropriate to rely on rope teammates to stop the fall of another teammate. However, when the surface conditions become firmer, a team needs to add running protection or belays for protection, as self-arrest becomes more difficult if not impossible. Belaying or adding intermediate protection during roped travel may also be prudent when the slope angle increases or the terrain below has greater consequences in the event of a fall (e.g., cliffs or crevasses below). Too many times, an entire rope team falls as a result of not being able to stop the fall of one teammate. (*Source: Denali Mountaineering Rangers.*)

INJURY WHILE DESCENDING GLACIAL MORAINE
Central Alaska Range, Granite Glacier

Three climbers flew to the Pika Glacier on July 16, spent a few days rock climbing in the Little Switzerland area, and began a traverse out of the mountains on July 19. The team had planned to return to Talkeetna on foot and by packraft. At approximately 6 p.m., while they were descending the boulder-strewn moraine of the lower Granite Glacier, a large boulder rolled over and caused one climber to fall on his left side and arm. A heavy backpack and the sharp corner of the boulder on which the patient landed resulted in an open left forearm fracture between the elbow and the wrist. The injury exposed bone and caused significant bleeding and intense pain. His teammates applied direct pressure to the bleed, treated the injury to the best of their abilities, and called for help using an inReach satellite device.

Ranger Tucker Chenoweth responded to this limb- and life-threatening injury, arriving at the scene by helicopter with pilot Andreas Hermansky at 9:45 p.m. Chenoweth treated the patient before evacuating the team to Talkeetna at 10:35 p.m. Chenoweth noted significant blood loss and decreased circulation, sensation, and motion of the patient's left arm. The patient was assessed by local ambulance providers and eventually was driven to the hospital by his climbing partners.

ANALYSIS
Unstable moraines require great care, especially with heavy backpacks. Trekking poles and a carefully loaded pack can help maintain balance, but some falls are almost inevitable. This patient was provided quality care by his teammates, who supported the injured extremity and slowed the bleeding. Without this field treatment, this climber could have lost his limb or his life while waiting for an evacuation. The value of wilderness medical training (and the means to contact rescuers in an emergency) cannot be overstated when traveling and climbing in remote areas. (*Source: Denali Mountaineering Rangers.*)

AVALANCHE
Eastern Alaska Range, Canwell Glacier

On March 26, a group from a University of Alaska Fairbanks introductory mountaineering class was out for its final climb. The class consisted of nine students (ages 20–28), one lead instructor, and three volunteer assistant instructors. After 11 weeks of class, including nine days of hands-on field time, the students were tasked with developing and executing a trip plan for their final group climb. The class chose a snow climb on the northwest face of McCallum Peak, off the Canwell Glacier in the eastern Alaska Range.

This trip would involve a six-mile approach to a proposed campsite at around 4,500 feet on a glacier on the north aspect of McCallum Peak. From there, the climb would consist of glacier travel and climbing on moderate snow slopes, up to 50°, to the summit at 6,700 feet. The students' plan was to leave early on Saturday to make the relatively flat approach to the campsite. If the avalanche conditions looked favorable, the plan was to wake up early on Sunday, climb the peak, descend back to camp, and then ski back out to the road.

The eastern Alaska Range has a classic cold and thin continental snowpack. The class had been into this area several times during the weeks preceding the climb, on similar aspects and elevations as the proposed climb. We spent quite a bit of time doing snow assessment during those trips, and at that time the stability was relatively good in most locations.

Ten days before the attempted climb, a storm came through this part of the Alaska Range, bringing about 70cm of new snow and approximately 25 mph winds. Directly after this storm, an advanced avalanche course was taught in the general area of our objective. The folks in this Avy 2 course shared high-quality snow observations on the Eastern Alaska Range Avalanche Center website, about a week before our climb. The snowpack showed an existing wind slab, a potential weak layer of facets, and a melt-freeze crust at 25cm depth. The test results showed poor stability,

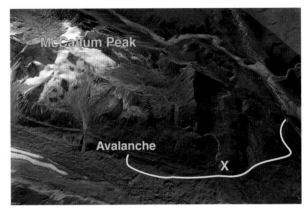

The climbers' route along the Canwell Glacier. The X marks the point where the group chose a lower route. They entered avalanche terrain while attempting to regain the high route. *Google Earth*

with easy initiation and high propagation potential. The avalanche course students and instructors identified "considerable" avalanche danger on all aspects above treeline.

The mountaineering course students and instructors had read and discussed the forecast and had identified avalanche conditions as the main hazard in a pre-trip meeting on Thursday. The class made a decision to mitigate this hazard by avoiding avalanche terrain until extensive observations and snowpack assessment were possible. The route the students planned to follow during the approach would keep the group almost completely out of avalanche terrain, and they chose a camp location that provided access to representative terrain for snowpack assessment.

The group got to the trailhead at 8:30 a.m. It was about 24°F. The temperatures had been in the 20s and 30s and clear, with 5–15 mph winds, since the storm the week before. After a quick trailhead talk and beacon check, the group headed out. Everyone was wearing a working beacon and a helmet. Everyone also had a shovel and a probe along with their camping and climbing gear. Throughout the course, we had done 12–15 hours of avalanche education, which included work in the classroom and in the field. Two of the instructors had their Avy 2 certifications, and three of the other members of the group had taken Avy 1 prior to the class.

During the approach, navigation was left to the students, and it proved to be challenging and time consuming. The group strayed off the trail along the moraine bench on the south side of the Canwell Glacier and ended up out on the glacier. The instructor let the students go the less efficient way to reinforce the lessons of route-finding and navigation that had been taught in the course. We had proceeded about 1.5 miles along the glacier before the students realized they wanted to be

Slab avalanche set off by climbers ascending toward the obvious moraine bench above.

on the large, flat moraine bench about 200 feet above them. The group gathered and briefly discussed the options, which were to retreat 1.5 miles to the find the spot that the group had headed out onto the glacier and then travel back along the trail, or else to find the best spot along the north-facing lateral moraine feature to climb up to the flats and trail above them. The group decided to find a way up the relatively short moraine slope in front of them instead of backtracking.

While grouped up, we also discussed the snowpack observations we had made so far that day. No one in the group had seen or heard any red flags up to that point. The folks in the lead chose a line that followed a snow ramp up along a shallow rock band on a 25–30° slope most of the way up the moraine feature. This line had one short section (40–50 feet) of 35–40° open snow slope at the top before reaching flat ground. Upon reaching this slope, the lead group strapped their skis on their packs and started up. The rest of the group went up the slope in a staggered line. For the first half of the slope, the snow consisted of 30cm of unconsolidated sugar over scree. About halfway up, the snow began to have a wind crust/slab that thickened toward the rollover from the flats above.

The lead people were about 20 feet from the flats above, and the last folks were about 100 feet below them, when the lead climber triggered a wind slab that entrained all 13 members of the climbing party. The two people in the lead only traveled a short distance downslope; five people were carried downslope but remained on top; four people were partially buried; and two people were completely buried close to the surface. The avalanche had an R3 relative size and a D2 destructive force. The crown was between 6 and 12 inches thick. The slide path was 150 feet wide at the top and 250 feet wide at the bottom, with 250-foot vertical fall.

After the slide, rescue was initiated by several of the unburied students. One student took lead and did a count, one student yelled to everyone to turn their beacons to search, and two other students began looking for clues and limbs sticking out of the snow. (This student-led rescue was necessary due to the fact that all of the instructors were either at the top of the slope or partially/fully buried.) Only one person was not accounted for right away—miraculous with 13 people involved in the slide. After a few seconds, this victim's fingers poked through the snow and were noticed by one of the students, who cleared the person's airway. Within 30 seconds, this person and all the others were being helped out of the snow. Two folks had minor breathing difficulties after their burial. Other noncritical injuries included a small leg laceration on one of the students, a small facial laceration from one student's sunglasses, and a minor hand laceration on one of the volunteer instructors. Several of the folks were cold from being buried and were given dry clothes and warmed up. After a brief discussion, the group packed up and skied several hours back to the vehicles.

ANALYSIS

Our group was extremely lucky that no one was seriously hurt or killed in this avalanche. The dangerous avalanche conditions persisted for the next couple of weeks. During that spring season, several human-triggered avalanches resulted in two fatalities within a few miles of our avalanche scene.

Here is a brief overview of some of the mistakes we made, contributing to our accident, along with strategies that we could have used to help mitigate the avalanche risks that we faced on our trip. This analysis is a combination of personal/in-house analysis in addition to a third-party assessment of the avalanche accident.

(1) *Poor decision-making and communication as a group.* The group didn't acknowledge a distinct terrain change (entering avalanche terrain for the first time that day) by grouping up and discussing all available options. We didn't follow the STOP rule: Stop, Think, Observe, Plan and Pre-Mortem. We didn't keep everyone informed and involved in the decision to get onto that particular slope. We didn't use a clear system for communication and decision-making.

(2) *Poor group management—putting everyone on the same slope.* We should have exposed only a minimum number of people to a hazard at one time.

(3) *Not being flexible enough with the trip plan.* We knew about the "considerable" avalanche risk and hoped to use terrain for protection instead of reconsidering the objective or changing the dates of the trip.

(4) *Avalanche blindness.* Had we been more sensitive to the hazard, we could have paused to acquire more information and/or backtracked to stay out of avalanche terrain completely.

(5) *Time constraints, feeling rushed.* We should have had more flexible time-management plans. (*Source: Lead instructor of the class.*)

ARIZONA

INJURY WHILE LEAPING CHASM
Sedona Area, Oak Creek Spire

On October 6, at approximately 3 p.m., the Coconino County Sheriff's Office received a 911 call from a climber (Person 1) who stated she had broken her leg and was hanging in her harness on the last pitch of Oak Creek Spire. It was determined that Person 1 was on the North Face/West Crack route. During the call, Person 1 stated that her climbing partner was going to maneuver her to a ledge so that she was not suspended from the rope. The weather was good, with air temperatures in the high 70s.

Rescuers from four agencies responded and determined that a helicopter short-haul was the best option. Person 1 was successfully short-hauled from a ledge to a staging area and then transferred to an ambulance for transport to the hospital.

Person 1 was interviewed at the hospital and indicated that this was the climbers' first attempt at this route. Person 1 (age 32) had 10 years of climbing experience and is comfortable leading 5.10 traditional routes, and Person 2 (27) had 15 years of climbing experience.

Person 1 was following Person 2 on the third pitch, during which the climbers must jump from a northern spire to the higher south spire. Person 1 stated that she was a little nervous about the move and consequently she jumped with "too much force." She was able to grab a hold with her hands but struck the rock with her feet and sustained a bimalleolar fracture (broken ankle) in her right leg. Person 2 assisted in belaying her to a ledge to await the rescue.

ANALYSIS

The nearly six-foot jump-across move on Oak Creek Spire has some inherent risk, as it is impossible to protect either the leader or the second against a hard landing if the jump is misjudged. Person 1 stated that she jumped with too much force, and she had some bad luck with striking her leg in a way that broke the ankle. It was helpful that the team had mobile phone service and thus was able to call promptly for a rescue, just a few hours before dark. (*Source: Aaron Dick, Coconino County Sheriff's Office.*)

The infamous jump move on the last pitch of Oak Creek Spire. *Larry Coats*

SWINGING FALL ON SPORT CLIMB
Jacks Canyon

Toward the end of a full day of climbing, a group headed to the Slot Machine, a prominent feature of the Casino Cliffs in Jacks Canyon. One climber, Person 3, attempted Slots O Fun, a 5.10a limestone sport route, approximately 35 feet high, with four bolts and a bolted anchor. Person 2 was belaying. Person 3 was able to place quickdraws on the first three bolts, but was unable to finish the climb.

Person 1, 32 years old and moderately experienced, then attempted the route, clipping the three preplaced quickdraws. As he moved beyond the third piece of protection, he climbed up and sideways. He was a full body length above and half a body length lateral to his last piece of protection when he slipped and fell approximately 15 feet. Person 2, a 26-year-old, moderately experienced climber, arrested his fall, but during the fall Person 1 caught his left foot on the rock and sustained an ankle ligament injury and fractured talus. A group of climbers carried Person 1 about a mile back to camp, and the climber sought treatment the next morning.

ANALYSIS

This route was above the skill level of the group, and after climbing all day the climbers were tired and their judgment was impaired; they would have been better off trying this route another day. Climbing laterally to the line of bolts resulted in a swinging fall and contributed to the mechanism of injury; remaining in line with the protection helps minimize this risk. The belayer also felt the "catch was not as soft as it should have been, accelerating the climber's collision with the wall." (*Source: Anonymous member of the climbing team.*)

CALIFORNIA

GLISSADING WITH CRAMPONS
Mt. Shasta, Avalanche Gulch

On June 11, a female climber was descending the Avalanche Gulch route. Once below the Red Banks, she attempted to glissade down snow toward Helen Lake. Somewhere near the Heart, her crampons caught in the snow or ice and she twisted or broke her ankle. Ranger Nick Meyers responded to her location, at about 11,700 feet, and assisted her down to Helen Lake, from which a California Highway Patrol helicopter transported her to Mercy Medical.

ANALYSIS
Glissading while wearing crampons is one of the leading causes of injury on Mt. Shasta. Don't do it. (*Source: Mt. Shasta and Castle Crags Wilderness Climbing Ranger Report 2016.*)

FALL FROM SUMMIT PINNACLE
Mt. Shasta

On June 22, shortly after noon, a 44-year-old man fell off the summit pinnacle of Mt. Shasta and sustained multiple injuries. Shasta Mountain Guides owner/operator Chris Carr and local physician Dr. Sean Malee were on the scene and handled patient care. Dr. Malee's report follows.

As the climb doc for the Breast Cancer Fund Climb Against the Odds, I was waiting on the summit for the last rope team of our group, led by Shasta Mountain Guides. Senior guide Rich Meyer observed an independent climber fall off the south side of the summit pinnacle. He fell approximately 25 feet vertically over rime-covered rock, then tumbled another 100 feet down firm, icy snow, coming to a rest on the summit plateau.

I descended on skis to reach the climber, who was one of several leaders of a large group of Boy Scouts that had ascended the east side of Mt. Shasta on a multi-day climb. I immediately made an assessment. The patient was complaining of a broken left arm and had no memory of the events after summiting. His head was covered with abrasions and blood, with a small laceration over his left eye. He also complained of back pain on his right side.

I dug out a level area and moved the patient to a stable position. Using emergency Mylar blankets and a bivy sack, as well as scavenged garments from other climbers, we insulated him from the snow to prevent hypothermia. Over the three-hour rescue we were blessed with warm sunshine, light winds, and ambient temperatures of around 35° to 40°F. Lead climbing ranger Nick Meyers eventually notified me that California Highway Patrol (CHP) helicopter H-14 was on the way. During the three hours we waited, the injured climber remained alert and oriented, with good vitals and warm extremities.

Near the limits of the CHP helicopter's altitude capabilities, the pilot made a heroic, full-power landing on the south side of the summit plateau, at approximately

13,800 feet, at 3 p.m. The rescuers carried the patient by his clothing and moved him into the helicopter behind the pilot's seat as quickly as possible. The pilot was able to lift off and descend directly to the hospital for definitive care. The patient's injuries included multiple spinal fractures, distal left forearm fracture, multiple rib fractures, pneumothorax, a traumatic liver injury, and abrasions to the head. Last word was that he was in stable condition and expected to make a good recovery.

ANALYSIS

I attributed the fall to fatigue, inexperience, and a lack of focus, given the exposed position he was in. (More concerning was the lack of preparation of the patient's entire group, given that the majority of them were youths and few to none were wearing helmets or carrying packs, many were clad all in cotton, and few had any spare layers of insulation.) Without the help of the experienced mountain guide who happened to be on scene and the pilot's "dicey" landing, the climber likely would have not survived the ordeal. (*Source: Dr. Sean Malee, Mt. Shasta and Castle Crags Wilderness Climbing Ranger Report 2016.*)

FALL ON SNOW | Painful Self-Rescue

Mt. Shasta, Avalanche Gulch

On July 25 at approximately 2:45 p.m., Bryan Bridgefs slipped and fell below Red Banks on the south side of Mt. Shasta. From his location at about 12,000 feet, Bridgefs called 911. Mike Burns from Siskiyou County Search and Rescue called climbing ranger Matt Dooley at 3:15 p.m. to explain the situation. He said Bridgefs had complained of arm pain and had reported that he was unable to move.

At approximately 4:15 p.m., a California Highway Patrol (CHP) helicopter began flying over the area. CHP soon located the injured Bridgefs, but due to warm temperatures limiting the helicopter's capabilities at higher elevations, they were unable to reach his location and pick him up. The helicopter landed in the Bunny Flat parking lot, and the pilot, Burns, and Dooley discussed their options. It would take a minimum of two hours to hike to the patient's location from Helen Lake. Twelve- to 18-inch-deep sun cups in the snow would limit the effectiveness of a lowering the climber in a sked (rescue stretcher), and the risk of rockfall to rescuers and the climber would be greater during the afternoon and evening. The CHP helicopter might be unable to reach Bridgefs before darkness. However, the helicopter would be able to make an extraction attempt early the next morning, if needed.

At approximately 4:45 p.m., Dooley and Burns consulted with Bridgefs by phone. Bridgefs was informed of the difficulties preventing a rescue that day and advised to do his best to keep descending on his own, despite pain that he reported was preventing him from taking more than a few steps at a time. His brother, Robert, would accompany him. The rescuers made plans for a morning mission if the patient was unable to self-rescue during the night.

At about 10 p.m., the injured Bridgefs arrived at Helen Lake and called Burns, who advised him to keep descending if he could. The patient reached the road at approximately 3 a.m. and soon checked in at Mercy Medical Center.

ANALYSIS

This incident is documented mainly to highlight the fact that self-rescue some-times may be the only option after an accident. Poor weather, darkness, and other factors may prevent a rescue team from reaching a patient. As a result, climbers on Shasta and other mountains must be prepared either to wait through the night for help to arrive (having carried appropriate clothing, shelter, food, water, first-aid and painkillers) or else be equipped and mentally prepared to self-evacuate. (*Source: Mt. Shasta and Castle Crags Wilderness Climbing Ranger Report 2016 and the Editors.*)

FALL FROM RED BANKS | Failure to Follow Route, Inexperience
Mt. Shasta, Avalanche Gulch

At 9:30 a.m. on August 11, I (Ranger Forrest Coots) re-ceived a call from Siskiyou County Search and Rescue coordinator Mike Burns while patrolling the lower elevations of the south side of Mt. Shasta. Officer Burns stated that a 911 call had come in for an injured male climber in Avalanche Gulch. The climber had fallen off the Red Banks and down the upper mountain, left of the Heart, at about 12,500 feet.

Avalanche Gulch with the Red Banks formation spanning the top left of the photo. The normal routes breach the Red Banks on their right side. *Nick Meyers*

Burns started the search for available aircraft, and California Highway Patrol (CHP) and Air National Guard helicopters responded out of Auburn and Sacramen-to. At noon, Burns received a call from a party who had downclimbed to the injured climber and stated that the climber was unconscious but breathing. At 12:30 p.m., the reporting party called back and said the injured climber might have stopped breathing.

The CHP helicopter H-24 landed at the Bunny Flat rescue cache at 1 p.m. and configured for lowering SAR members to the scene. However, winds prevented this operation. At 1:55 p.m., the Air National Guard's Spartan 630 arrived at Bunny Flat and successfully performed a hoist. The injured climber was transported to Mercy Medical Center in Mt. Shasta, where he was pronounced dead.

ANALYSIS

This climbing party was a father and son team. The father, 53, had some mountain-eering experience, but the teenage son had never climbed. Other climbers on the mountain described the father and son ascending left of the Heart and attempting a much more difficult and dangerous route than usual through the Red Banks. The thin, icy gullies or chimneys through very loose pumice on the left side of the Red Banks are rarely climbed, and for good reason. The son was able to climb one of the ice chimneys, and he waited at the top for his father. As the older man was reach-ing the top of the chimney, the son heard his dad yell and saw him fall through the chimney and slide approximately 500 feet before coming to rest.

These two climbers were inexperienced and off route. The easier routes around the right side of the Red Banks formation are easily viewed from below, so it is unknown why these climbers chose to attempt the loose and more technical ice chimney. (*Source: Ranger Forrest Coots, Mt. Shasta and Castle Crags Wilderness Climbing Ranger Report 2016.*)

CLEAR CREEK ROUTE FATALITY: *There was one other climbing fatality on Mt. Shasta during the 2016 season. On July 3, a 76-year-old man fell at approximately 9,600 feet on the Clear Creek Route, failed to self-arrest, and slid into a rock. The patient died from his injuries that night.*

GROUND FALL | Cams Pulled Out
South Lake Tahoe, Pie Shop

My wife and I were climbing at Pie Shop, a granite crag in South Lake Tahoe where we had been multiple times. I was leading the first pitch of True Grip, a right-angling 5.10b finger crack. While I am an experienced trad leader and have comfortably climbed many routes at this grade, my finger-crack skills were a known weakness. Nonetheless, the protection potential was better on this climb than on two 5.10 climbs I had just top-roped, and I assessed it as sufficiently safe to lead.

I fell off while attempting the opening moves, and my wife (belayer) spotted my fall. I quickly got back on the climb and worked my way up to the first solid finger lock and put in a blue TCU; I didn't use a quickdraw since I was close to the ground. I moved up the climb, ultimately placing three more pieces: blue and gray TCUs without draws, then a gray TCU with an alpine draw. (*Editor's note: The gray 00 Metolius TCU is the second-smallest in the TCU line. The blue number 1 TCU is designed for half-inch to two-thirds-inch cracks.*) I inspected and pull-tested all the placements and believed they were sound. However, I was shaky on the lead, unable to find good rest positions and not confident in my feet.

As I moved above my last piece of protection, I saw a decent foothold on my left, one move higher, so I stepped up and tried to get to a rest position. However, I was unable to secure good finger locks and I believe my foot slipped. I was about a body length above my last piece of protection (the gray TCU) and approximately 25 feet up the wall.

As I fell, three pieces of protection pulled (the first, third, and fourth) and I hit the ground. The majority of the blow in striking the ground was absorbed on the left side of my lower and middle back, which impacted a manzanita stump. The wind was knocked out of me. After my breathing returned to normal, my wife and I did a high-level injury assessment: My back and rib cage hurt where I hit the stump but were not exceedingly painful; my left wrist was sore; and I had a handful of small abrasions. After determining that I did not appear to have any head or spine injuries or puncture wounds, my wife helped me up and packed our gear, and we slowly hiked out to the car and drove to the ER.

I was diagnosed with four transverse process fractures of the vertebrae, two broken ribs, and a minor collapse of the left lung. A month later, an MRI revealed that I also had suffered a broken left wrist. Fortunately, all injuries have fully healed and I have returned to climbing. And I am working on my finger-crack technique.

ESSENTIALS

MICRO-CAMS
WHAT TO EXPECT, HOW TO OPTIMIZE
By the Editors

Tiny cams pulling out of cracks frequently contribute to accidents reported in these pages. Often, these cams are deformed by twisting and impact forces, leading climbers to conclude the units have "failed," when the real culprit is almost always unrealistic expectations of the capabilities of micro-cams and/or less than optimal placements.

Micro-cams are defined here as smaller than 2/3 inch (17mm) at their widest range—such cams' effective range maxes out at around 1/2 inch (13mm) or fingertip size. These cams are rated to significantly lower strength than their larger siblings (up to 50 percent less). More significantly, the smaller surface area of each cam lobe and their limited expansion range make micro-cams much more likely to shear or pull out of a crack if the placement is not optimal.

Many times, a wired nut can be placed in the same spot as an equivalent size cam and will be easier to evaluate and more predictable. With practice, nuts can be placed almost as quickly as cams. If a micro-cam must be used, optimize the piece's security in these ways:

- *Choose the best placement.* Whenever possible, place small cams toward the bottom of flares or constrictions, so they benefit from passive resistance to pulling out, like a nut. Even "parallel" cracks may have subtle variations.
- *Avoid dirty, sandy, wet, icy, loose, or soft rock.*
- *Set cams in the narrower half of their range.* In terms of security, there is no such thing as an "over-cammed" micro-cam.
- *Try to prevent cams from walking out of place.* Look for nubbins or variations in the crack that will hold the cam in its best position. Extend the placement with a quickdraw or sling to keep the rope from moving it. Avoid knocking the cam out of place with your hand, foot, body, or equipment.
- *Orient the cam stem in the anticipated direction of pull.* Cams that rotate under load put more force on fewer cam lobes.
- *Double up on dubious placements.* Avoid having "all your eggs in one basket" with micro-cams.

There is no guaranteed bomber placement in nature. In the words of guide and author Topher Donahue, "Every placement is only as good as the judgment of the person who placed it, on the day they placed it."

With information from Rob Coppolillo, Topher Donahue, Jim Karn, Dale Remsberg, and Rick Vance.

A solid small cam placed in good, dry rock, in the tighter half of the unit's range, at the bottom of a constriction, with the stem oriented in the direction of anticipated pull. Ideally, the cam might be placed a little deeper into the crack, so the outer lobes aren't as close to the edge. *NPS Photo*

ANALYSIS

The fall happened very quickly, but the gear that pulled may have absorbed some of the energy of the fall, or else I believe that I would have been more seriously injured. The top TCU was substantially deformed, and the metal lobes of each of the TCUs that pulled showed significant shearing where they had been in contact with the rock. There were no issues with the rope or belay. Overall, the force of the fall was just too great for the size and quantity of protection. With smaller gear, there is much less margin for error. Just slight walking of a small cam can greatly reduce the force it may hold. My key takeaway is to place protection more often when using small gear, doubling up on the really small pro and/or adding big gear soon afterward, if possible. Finally, knowing that finger-crack technique was a weakness, I should have approached this route as a project versus an onsight. (*Source: Tim Maly.*)

LEDGE FALL | Inadequate Protection
Yosemite Valley, Church Bowl

On April 16, at about 3 p.m., Yosemite Dispatch received a report of a climber who had taken a lead fall and was bleeding severely at Church Bowl. The climber (male, age 24) had pulled multiple pieces of protection from the Bishop's Terrace route (5.8) and landed on a ledge 20 feet above the ground. An advanced life support provider arrived on scene, meeting an off-duty ranger who happened to be climbing in the area. The climber's partner stated that the fall had been approximately 25 feet and that the climber had hit his head during the fall. He lost consciousness for approximately three minutes. He was wearing a helmet. The two care providers climbed to the patient, assessed his injuries, and moved the patient to the base of the climb. A Yosemite Valley ambulance then took the patient to El Cap Meadow and transferred care to Mercy Air Ambulance.

ANALYSIS

When climbing above a ledge or in low-angle terrain, it is particularly important to place gear early and often. Don't just think about the piece right below you—consider the consequences if that piece fails. Would the next piece keep you off the ledge below? (*Source: Yosemite National Park Climbing Rangers.*)

RAPPEL ERROR | Damaging Pendulum Swing
Yosemite Valley, Royal Arches Area

On May 3, at approximately 11:30 p.m., a climber notified park rangers that his climbing partner might have sustained a broken leg during a rappelling accident while descending from the route Sons of Yesterday. The patient was located on a belay ledge at the start of the second pitch of the route Super Slide, to climber's left of Sons of Yesterday. A decision was made to rescue the patient at first light the next day, as it was considered unsafe to initiate a technical rescue at that time.

At about 8:15 the next morning, a first responder reached the patient, who was alert and oriented, and stated that he had swung into a wall and impacted with his arm and leg while rappelling. His chief complaint was the pain from his leg injury; his upper leg was swollen. After providing patient care and establishing fixed lines to the location, the team lowered the patient, packaged in a rigid litter, to the ground. The rescue team then did a carry-out to the Ahwahnee parking area and transferred care to the Valley ambulance.

ANALYSIS

A debrief of the incident revealed that the injury occurred while the climbers were rappelling from an anchor on Sons of Yesterday to the top anchor of Serenity Crack. (*Sons of Yesterday begins above the third pitch of Serenity Crack.*) If intermediate rappel stations are skipped here, this rappel requires tensioning hard to the right on a blank face. Left of the fall line is a large drop-off. The patient lost control of his footing, which sent him into a pendulum over the drop-off at a rate of speed high enough to result in a broken femur and wrist. Use of an intermediate rappel station removes the need to tension so far to the right on rappel.

As a climber tried to rappel from point A to B, he slipped and pendulumed violently to the left over the large shaded corner. *Steph Abegg*

We later spoke with another climber who had lost control of his rappel in the same spot and also swung around the corner. As climbers we sometimes underestimate the force of an out-of-control pendulum. Always watch the angle of deflection from your upper anchor and ask yourself: Am I willing to risk a downward fall in this terrain? A pendulum can generate the same amount of force as falling straight down, and exposes a larger, more vulnerable section of the body to impact.

Lastly, this incident is a great reminder of the importance of a no-hands backup in any rappel system. This climber's backup helped him maintain control even after sustaining serious injuries, allowing him to continue lowering himself to the ledge on which he was found. It may well have saved his life. (*Source: Yosemite National Park Climbing Rangers.*)

DROPPED HAUL BAG BREAKS CLIMBER'S ARM
Yosemite Valley, El Capitan

On June 16, at approximately 12:30 p.m., Yosemite Dispatch received a 911 call about a climber injury on El Capitan in the vicinity of the Heart Ledges rappels. Pete, Mark, and Vlad had just finished climbing Little John Right, a three- to four-pitch 5.8 route at the base of the west wall of El Capitan. (*The names of all climbers have been changed in this report.*) While Vlad was belaying Pete to the top of the climb, Mark began setting up a rappel from the bolted anchors on the left side of the pinnacle. Vlad and Pete joined him at the rappel station as Mark headed down. Upon reaching the ground, Mark yelled, "Off rappel!" to his partners. Very shortly after this, Vlad and Pete heard "HAUL BAG, HAUL BAG, HAUL BAG!!!" screamed from above. Vlad, who had already rigged for rappel, pressed flat against the wall. Vlad remembers that Pete was sitting and unable to move out of the way quickly, and he was hit in the left arm by a fully loaded haul bag.

The haul bag came from a party above that was rappelling from Heart Ledges, retreating due to time constraints. This party consisted of climbers Jeff and Aaron. At the time of the incident, Aaron was on the final rappel and getting close to the level of Little John pinnacle. Jeff, who had been rappelling with the haul bag, was one rappel higher and about 100 feet above Little John pinnacle.

Upon seeing what happened, Aaron, who is a wilderness first responder (WFR), swung hard to the right to reach the ledge and immediately began assisting. Jeff, who is an emergency medical technician (EMT), hastily rappelled to the ledge and began helping as well. Mark and Aaron had cell phones but initially could not get service; eventually Aaron managed to call 911, which patched him through to YOSAR.

On the ledge, the party's main concern was to control bleeding from Pete's left arm, which appeared to have suffered a severe, open fracture of the humerus. Initial attempts at direct pressure failed to stop the hemorrhaging, so the team attempted to tourniquet Pete's arm, first with a shirt and then with a sling. [*Editor's note: Direct pressure should be applied for five minutes on all wounds except those that are spurting (indicative of an arterial bleed) or bleeding extremely rapidly. Use of a sling for a tourniquet should be a last resort. Narrow (less than 1.5 inches), unpadded material is generally ineffective and will cause tissue damage and complicate surgical repair.*] The tourniquet was unsuccessful, but eventually they managed to control the bleeding using continuous direct pressure with clothing. Due to the unstable nature of the injury and the bleeding, the team decided to wait until YOSAR arrived instead of attempting a self-extrication. Jeff did a patient assessment and found nothing significant beyond the extreme trauma to the patient's left arm. While waiting on the ledge, the team continued to check CSM (circulation, sensation, motion) in Pete's left arm every five minutes.

[Left] Mockup of the rigging used to rappel with a haul bag on El Capitan. The locking carabiner clipped to the yellow slings (connecting the haul bag to the rappel carabiner) is believed to have unclipped in the Yosemite incident. Including the haul bag connection (not shown), this setup used seven carabiners. [Right] A much simpler setup with a doubled cordelette to connect the rappel device to both the climber and the haul bag (gray slings), using only two carabiners.

At approximately 12:55 p.m., a "hasty team" of park rangers arrived at the base. They informed the climbers that a technical team and advanced life support was en route, but it would likely take at least an hour for them to get into position and complete a rescue lower. With this information, the group decided to stabilize Pete's arm as best they could, using shirts, hiking poles, and materials from Aaron's first-aid kit, and rappel with Pete to the ground to meet the rescue team.

After packaging Pete's arm, Jeff rigged for a tandem rappel using a modified version of a rescue spider, a rappel configuration that allowed Jeff to rappel down the line along with Pete, carrying Pete's weight on the rappel device. (It should be noted that this was essentially the same method Jeff had used to rappel with the haul bag that dropped; with various iterations, it is a common way to rappel with a heavy load.) As Jeff and Pete reached the base, the full rescue team arrived. YOSAR paramedics assessed Pete and repackaged his arm. After an initial attempt at an assisted walkout, it was decided to package Pete into a litter and carry him down the trail. He was flown in a medical helicopter from El Cap Meadow.

ANALYSIS

Jeff had been rappelling with an ATC extended from his harness on two Purcell prusiks. These were each clipped separately to a locking carabiner (the master-point) that was holding his rappel device. His rappel was backed up by a prusik hitch on the rope below his ATC.

To carry the haul bag, Jeff had clipped another locking carabiner to the master point, clipped a sling to this, and clipped the sling to the haul bag. He clipped a second sling from the haul bag directly to the same locker that was clipped to the masterpoint. (See photo at left.) Each sling was attached at the haul bag with an individual non-locking carabiner, and the two were opposite and opposed.

While some specifics were lost in the chaos or simply could not be recalled, it is known that, while Jeff was rappelling, the haul bag caught on a small ledge. This caused the slings holding the bag to go slack temporarily. When the bag released from the ledge, it somehow unclipped from the masterpoint and dropped.

Although no one in either team was 100 percent sure, they are fairly certain that when the bag landed on Little John, both runners were attached to the haul bag. This would mean the failure point was at the locking carabiner clipped into the masterpoint. Jeff believes the locker that was holding the two runners going to his haul bag opened and simultaneously released the two attachment points. Whether he failed to lock it before starting down or it unlocked during the rappel due to vibration and improper orientation is unknown.

The fact that multiple people involved in this incident had medical training and/or self-rescue knowledge was critical to saving Pete's arm and his life.

Other takeaways from this incident:

- Always check that your locking carabiners are locked, and periodically double-check that they've *stayed* locked.
- Although Jeff's basic system for rappelling with the haul bag was properly configured, there are simpler ways to rig this rappel. The number of carabiners in Jeff's rigging may have contributed to a failure to recognize the unlocked carabiner. Simplicity is an element of safe climbing systems.
- Be constantly aware of your surroundings while climbing. Parties climbing and rappelling above you are always a cause for concern.
- Yelling "ROCK!" loudly and repeatedly is the best way to get the attention of people below. The climbers could have been momentarily confused by the yelled words "haul bag." (*Source: Yosemite National Park Climbing Rangers.*)

SIMUL-RAPPEL FAILURE | No Backups
Yosemite Valley, Reed's Pinnacle

The names of the climbers in this report have been changed. On July 10, at 2:50 p.m., Yosemite Dispatch received a call regarding a climber fall with injuries at Reed's Pinnacle. The initial reports came in as a male climber with a broken leg. Upon arrival at the parking area, the first responding ranger found an adult male, John, 33, with an angulated lower leg/ankle fracture. John told the ranger that his partner David, age 41, was still at the base of the cliff and had been in and out of consciousness after a long fall.

The park ranger ran up the approach trail to the base of the cliff with a medic bag. Upon reaching the cliff, he found David unresponsive, without a pulse, and not breathing. He immediately called for additional resources and began CPR. After updates and communication with the park's Medical Control, the patient was pronounced dead at approximately 3:55 p.m.

Numerous interviews with the surviving climber and post-accident analysis by the responding ranger revealed some details of what had happened. Before the accident, the two climbers had climbed Lunatic Fringe, a popular 5.10c single-pitch route. After leading, John remained at the anchor at the top of the climb to belay David up. The two climbers then decided to simul-rappel, with each climber rappelling one strand of the rappel rope, so that each climber would counterweight the other. David used a Petzl Grigri, while John used a Black Diamond ATC device. They were using an 80-meter rope, both ends of which reached the ground from this anchor, but without any extra.

During the rappel, John was beneath David and remembers David stopping or slowing down at some point. John reached a small, sloping ledge about 15 feet above the ground and waited for David to catch up with him. According to the post-accident analysis, David was roughly 70 feet off the ground at this point. John felt a sudden change in the pull of the rope and the rope "going," and he started to fall. He briefly lost consciousness, and when he came to he saw David on the ground near him. John asked David if he was OK and remembered David briefly responding. John told David that he would go get help. When he tried to stand, he realized his leg was broken, and so he crawled down the short approach. At the Reed's parking area, he found visitors who were able to call 911, activating Yosemite's emergency response.

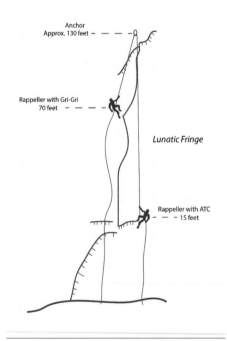

ANALYSIS
From a follow-up investigation, it is believed David fell approximately 70 feet after the end of the rope on John's side passed through John's ATC rappel de-

Relative positions of the two climbers in a Reed's Pinnacle simul-climbing accident. *NPS Diagram*

vice. This was determined based on the amount of rope left beneath David's Grigri as well as other observations. There were no knots or backup systems on the rope.

A fixed nut was observed in the crack near the point where David fell, and one possible explanation is that David paused to attempt to remove this piece of equipment. If David had pulled onto a stance momentarily, unweighting his side of the rope, John would have felt himself suddenly drop (as he stated consistently). It's possible this caused John to lose control of his side of the rappel rope. Without a hands-free backup hitch (e.g., autoblock), he would not have been able to regain control of the rope as it rapidly passed through his belay device, causing both men to fall to the ground.

Simul-rappelling is an advanced technique that is rarely required by the average climber. While simul-rappelling, both climber's lives are placed at risk by any mistakes. [Editor's note: Two climbers were seriously injured in another simul-rappelling accident, in the Shawangunks in New York, in 2016.]

John stated that one reason they decided to simul-rappel was that David had a Grigri, which can only be used to rappel a single strand of rope. To avoid the risk incurred by simul-rappelling, John and David could have tied the rope to the anchor, allowing David to rappel the fixed rope on his Grigri. John then could have untied the fixed rope and rappelled with his ATC as usual. (Controlling a rappel with an ATC is patently safer with two strands of rope as opposed to one.) Moreover, David reportedly had climbed the route before and knew the climbers could rappel the route with a single 80-meter rope. Knowing this, David could have lowered John to the ground after he led the pitch, and then John could have belayed David on a top-rope as he seconded the route.

In the special circumstances that simul-rappelling is preferred, good communication is essential. The excessive distance (about 50 feet) between the two climbers perhaps inhibited David from expressing to John that he planned to slow or stop his rappel. If John had been nearer to David, he may have had the opportunity to anticipate the momentary weight shift and not lose control of his device.

One or more backup systems could have prevented this accident. Stopper knots in the ends of the rope would have prevented the rope from passing through John's rappel device. A "hands-free" backup, such as a friction hitch, also might have prevented the catastrophic loss of control. Finally, the two climbers could have linked themselves with a tether, in effect closing the system until they both reached the ground. (Source: Yosemite National Park Climbing Rangers.)

RAPPEL ERROR | Attempted to Rappel Unanchored Rope
Yosemite Valley, El Capitan, East Ledges Descent

Christopher Vale and his partner Luke started climbing the west face of El Capitan around 7:30 a.m. on September 5. (*The name of Vale's climbing partner has been changed.*) The two had met a few days earlier and climbed the Steck-Salathé on Sentinel Rock as a warmup for El Capitan. They finished the west face on El Cap at around 7 p.m. After topping out, Vale was in a hurry to get back down. (He had plans to go back up on El Capitan the next day to work on Free Rider.) By 8 p.m., the two climbers had descended to the top of the East Ledges rappels.

Vale reached the rappels first and began descending while Luke was still a little ways behind. At the time of their descent, other climbers had left ropes in place for the four rappels. When Luke reached the rappels, he could see Vale's headlamp descending below. Luke heard Vale yell "off rappel." Approximately eight seconds later, Luke heard crashing and saw that Vale's headlamp had disappeared. Luke recognized that his partner had taken a large fall and tried to establish communication with him. Unable to get a response, Luke called 911 to activate a rescue.

Yosemite Search and Rescue dispatched a hasty team up the trail to make contact with the party. Upon arrival at the bottom of the East Ledges rappels, the SAR team found the patient showing no signs of life. After consultation with Park Medical Control, the climber was declared deceased.

ANALYSIS

The East Ledges rappel route descends a vertical cliff approximately 500 feet high. Most climbing teams complete this descent with rappels via bolted anchors. Multiple trees exist on the cliff between the bolted anchors.

Before Vale's fall, ropes had been fixed along the rappel route. These fixed ropes were of unknown origin but were being used regularly by climbers to expedite their descent and for ascending to the top of the wall to access routes from above. Climbers who had descended the East Ledges in the days prior to Vale's fall said they had seen a blue rope hanging adjacent to the standard rappel route and stuck in a flake and tree. In daylight, the climbers said, it was obvious that this rope was "garbage" and was not safe to use, but this fact must not have been easily observed at night.

When YOSAR arrived on scene, they observed a blue rope rigged through Vale's ATC rappel device. While it is impossible to know the exact sequence of events that preceded Vale's fall, it is likely that he arrived at a ledge between the first and second anchors from the top, saw the blue rope in the tree to his right, and considered it to be the next rappel line. He removed his ATC from the first line, called "off rappel" to his partner above, and rigged his ATC onto the blue rope. At some point while he was weighting the blue line, the rope dislodged and Vale fell to the base of the rappels.

Avoid rappelling or ascending ropes unless the condition and security of the rope, including its anchor, is known. In the dark and in a hurry, it is reasonable to assume that Vale didn't inspect the blue line before committing his life to it.

Always test a new critical connection before undoing your previous connection. For example, after loading your rappel device, you should test-weight the rope while still connected to a trusted anchor.

Slow down. Check that your anchor is secure, your carabiners are locked, and that your device is loaded correctly before each rappel. No amount of time saved is worth skipping these steps.

The climb is not over until you're on the ground. Of the six climbing-related fatalities in Yosemite over the last two years, all have been related to rappelling and descending. Stay vigilant until you are completely done with your adventure. (Source: Yosemite National Park Climbing Rangers.)

LEADER FALL | Protection Pulled Out
Yosemite Valley, Washington Column

The names of the climbers in this report have been changed. On October 7, Mike and Dylan started up the South Face (5.8 C1) of Washington Column. The two had done a little climbing together, but never in Yosemite Valley and mostly on single-pitch climbs. Mike was the more experienced of the two, having done a number of Yosemite big-wall climbs, including routes on El Capitan. Dylan was newer to climbing, having started about one year before.

The team hiked their gear to the base of the route and started climbing in late morning. At the top of pitch one is a large ledge. Mike started up pitch two, a pin-scarred corner rated C1. Approximately 35 feet up, the piece Mike was standing on pulled out. Dylan and Mike believe he pulled out an additional three pieces of gear during his fall, before landing on the belay ledge on his right side.

When he tried to move, Mike experienced excruciating pain on his side and was having trouble breathing. The two realized that moving Mike on their own was likely impossible and they called 911. YOSAR sent a paramedic straight to the climber while the rest of the team prepared for a rescue. Although Mike was breathing regularly while lying on the ledge, any movement dramatically increased his pain. Because of

Accident scene on Washington Column. Three to four pieces pulled out during the leader's fall. *NPS Photo*

this, a helicopter short-haul extrication was deemed preferable over a traditional rope lower and litter carry-out. After a reconnaissance flight of the area, a ranger was inserted onto the ledge at about 5 p.m. and extracted Mike in the litter. Dylan descended with the SAR team.

ANALYSIS

First climbed in 1964, the crack systems of the South Face Route were heavily scarred by repeated piton placements. The typically shallow and flaring nature of these features can make protection in them less secure and harder to gauge than a normal crack placement. Seeing the inverted lobes on the first cam that pulled out, our best guess is that the cam failed because it was either under-cammed (piece too small for the placement) or placed in a flare.

Although it's impossible to know for sure, we also speculate that Mike placed the cam straight in as opposed to angling downward in the direction of the anticipated pull, because only two lobes of the cam were damaged. A cam placed straight in will distribute a disproportionate amount of force to the upper lobes, in this case possibly resulting in their failure.

In overhanging terrain, Mike's fall might have ended up fine. But when climbing above ledges or in low-angle terrain, place solid gear early and often. (*Source: Yosemite National Park Climbing Rangers.*)

LEADER FALL | Off Route, Inadequate Protection
Yosemite National Park, Cathedral Peak, Southeast Buttress

On July 17, at 9 a.m., Yosemite Dispatch received a call from a distressed party at the base of Cathedral Peak. The caller's 38-year-old male climbing partner had fallen while off route on the first pitch of the Southeast Buttress Route (5.6). The leader's right ankle appeared to be broken.

Prior to the fall, the leader had begun what he thought was the standard start to the route. Feeling that he was off route, he traversed left 20 feet in an attempt to gain easier ground. When this did not provide more moderate climbing, the patient attempted to reverse his traverse and fell. Because of the location of his last piece of protection, the climber not only took a long fall but also pendulumed across the face. The total length of the fall was estimated at 30 to 40 feet in low-angle terrain.

Due to limited park resources at the time and the open access at the base of the cliff, the rescue team decided to extract the patient via short haul with a helicopter as opposed to a long carry-out in a litter.

ANALYSIS

This very popular climb has several alternative starts, and as with most alpine routes it can be challenging to find and stay on the easiest line. Study the proposed route during the approach and from the base to gain perspective.

Cathedral Peak's popular Southeast Buttress Route (facing camera) has many variations. *Jordan Ramey*

On low-angle terrain, especially when the difficulty is modest, it's easy to move quickly far away from your last protection. Yet even a short fall on low-angle ground can be dangerous because of the likelihood of impacting ledges. Be vigilant about where and how often you place gear, and protect against swinging falls that expose the head and fragile organs to greater risk. Before you climb into unknown terrain, ask yourself, "Can I safely reverse these moves?" If not, try another line. (*Sources: Yosemite National Park Climbing Rangers and the Editors.*)

ANOTHER CATHEDRAL PEAK LEDGE FALL: *On August 5, a female climber in her mid-20s took a fall on the fourth pitch of the Southeast Buttress Route while attempting to pass other climbers with a 5.9 variation. Her single piece of protection pulled out in the fall, and she injured both ankles (breaking one) when she impacted the belay ledge. The climber and her partner were able to self-rescue to the base of the peak by rappelling, then called for a rescue. Tuolumne SAR arranged for a helicopter short haul to extract the patient.*

LEADER FALL | Inadequate Protection
Yosemite National Park, Tuolumne Meadows, Daff Dome

Around midday on August 12, a climbing party on Crescent Arch (5.10a) on Daff Dome reported that the 48-year-old, male leader had taken a 25-foot fall and sustained a dislocated shoulder and what appeared to be a broken ankle. It was reported that the belayer was pulled up while catching the fall and may have been slightly injured.

While climbing the second pitch of the route, the leader had reached a stance and placed a nut, but he was unhappy with the placement. While trying to remove the nut and find a better placement, he lost his balance and fell. He attempted to catch himself and dislocated his shoulder from the sudden jolt. About 10 feet below he hit a ledge, resulting in the ankle injury, then fell about 15 feet farther before his rope arrested him.

A team climbing above saw the accident, fixed their ropes, rappelled down, and assisted the leader as his partner lowered him to the first big ledge they could reach. They decided to wait there for SAR, which had already been contacted and was en route. The Tuolumne SAR team ascended to the patient, provided care, and lowered him to the ground.

ANALYSIS

The leader was almost 10 feet above his last piece when he was struggling to replace the nut. One option that might have prevented this accident would have been to clip the rope to the first nut, even if it wasn't perfect, and then work on a new piece of protection, only removing or re-placing the original piece once a better piece was clipped. (*Source: Yosemite National Park Climbing Rangers.*)

PENDULUM FALL DURING RAPPEL RETREAT | Thunderstorm
Yosemite National Park, Matthes Crest

Will and James started climbing Matthes Crest in the late morning on September 11. Both have spent decades climbing in the Sierra. (*Their names have been changed here.*) The day had started out with clear blue skies, and both climbers felt that the weather report promised stable enough conditions to proceed with the climb.

After the initial steep pitches, the team began to simul-climb through easier terrain on the ridge traverse. As they were climbing, clouds started to form. Quickly, the weather worsened to hail and lightning, prompting them to rappel from the ridge.

The first three rappels went well. The team found in-place anchors from previous teams and backed up the rappels with extra gear when necessary. At the fourth rappel Will went first. He saw an anchor far to one side but felt the slick rock would make it a difficult and risky rappel. Instead he rappelled down an angled corner to reach a stance and build his own rappel anchor. Will called "off rappel" and James began to rappel. He started straight down and then tried to tension over to the belay when he was even with Will. Before he could reach the anchor, James lost control of his footing and pendulumed "approximately 30 feet." He sustained traumatic injuries to both legs while swinging horizontally across the low-angle terrain.

The Matthes Crest. *NPS Photo*

James threw the ends of his rappel ropes to Will, who then pulled him over to the anchor. With James in extreme pain and unable to function at full capacity, Will lowered James to the ground and then rappelled to the base himself.

The two were getting wet, and temperatures were dropping. With no phone reception to call for help, they decided to send Will out to the front country to seek a rescue. Will left most of their clothing, food, and water with James to keep him as comfortable as possible; luckily, this included a rain jacket. James cut the bottom out of a backpack and slipped it over his legs to create an extra layer of protection from the elements. Will then jogged approximately five miles to the road and went directly to the Tuolumne SAR site, at about 8 p.m., to initiate a rescue.

Using GPS coordinates from his phone, Will was able to give the SAR team James' precise location. YOSAR sent a hasty team, including a registered nurse and a paramedic, to care for James until the helicopter could arrive with first light the next morning.

ANALYSIS

Being prepared for sudden changes in the weather is essential in the High Sierra. Although James' fractured heels were his only injuries, the potential for hypothermia was very real. Temperatures that night were in the low 30s (F). James wore only a long-sleeve fleece, but Will had carried a Gore-Tex jacket that may have prevented James from becoming hypothermic. Their clever improvisation of turning a backpack into a bivy sack was also important for maintaining James' warmth.

One way to avoid James' swinging fall would have been for Will to fix the rappel lines to the lower anchor after anchoring himself. James then could have rappelled more directly to the belay. Fixing the ropes at the lower anchor also acts as a backup for the second person—a good practice even on straight-down rappels.

James and Will both were using hands-free backups while rappelling. If James had let go of the rope during his fall or hit his head and been knocked out, his prusik would have arrested a catastrophic fall. Backups are especially important in a forced retreat like this, when contending with the extra hazards of rain, chill, loose rock, and haste. (*Source: Yosemite National Park Climbing Rangers.*)

UNROPED FALL FROM ALPINE RIDGE
Sierra Nevada, Bear Creek Spire

On the afternoon of September 18, a two-person party was near the summit of Bear Creek Spire (13,726 feet) after climbing the east ridge, one of the longest routes in the Sierra (5.8 and more than 20 pitches, if the entire route is belayed). Although the party carried a rope and had used it for some of the more difficult sections of the route, they were unroped as they approached the summit. Leading the way was Maria Birukova, a 26-year-old, experienced climber with a number of California alpine routes under her belt. A large portion of rock "broke from under her feet" and she fell approximately 800 to 1,000 feet. Her body was recovered by search and rescue personnel two days later. (*Sources: Inyo County SAR report, Supertopo, Rock and Ice.*)

ANALYSIS

This is the first report we've published about an accident on the east ridge of Bear Creek Spire. Although regarded as a good route, it's not as popular as the peak's northeast ridge or the north arête, and a number of trip reports note the rock quality being poorer than on the more popular lines. The terrain was well within the victim's abilities and experience level. It's possible that incoming weather or the lateness of the day influenced the climbers' decisions to climb unroped through relatively easy terrain.

The "Kiwi coil" shortens the rope while maintaining a strong connection to the harness. There are several variations, but all of them tie off the coils to the belay loop.

Long alpine ridges frequently require altnernating between a number of techniques, including climbing unroped, simul-climbing, and belaying individual pitches. There are risks with each approach, and climbers must balance the relative safety of each versus the pressures of time and weather as they move up a route. Shortening the rope with a "Kiwi coil" (see photo) can allow climbers to move together over complex terrain and still place intermediate protection or use natural features for protection against a catastrophic fall, without creating excess rope drag or rockfall danger. Some trip reports indicate the final section of Bear Creek Spire's east ridge can be climbed using a "picket fence" method to weave the rope among natural rock features, protecting to a degree. (*Source: The Editors.*)

FATAL UNROPED FALLS ON EVOLUTION TRAVERSE AND IN KINGS CANYON NATIONAL PARK: *In early September, Julia Mackenzie, 30, fell during an attempt on the Evolution Traverse, likely because of a loose hold. She was climbing with a partner but was unroped. In mid-September, Alfred Kwok, 50, was discovered to have fallen on the upper southwest face of Deerhorn Mountain during a solo backcountry trip. The exact circumstances of these fatal falls are not known.*

LONG LEADER FALL | Loose Hold, Inadequate Protection
Sierra Nevada, Palisades, Temple Crag

At approximately 6:30 p.m. on July 3, a two-person team began climbing the 15th pitch (5.4) of the 18- to 22-pitch route Sun Ribbon Arête (5.10a) on Temple Crag (12,999 feet). Just prior to arriving at the notch belay at the top of the pitch, the leader (female, 28) pulled on a loose rock and dislodged it. The leader fell approximately 60 feet and was held by a 0.75 Black Diamond Camalot once the belayer (male, 29) arrested the fall. The leader sustained a broken toe and sprained left ankle and broke the fifth digit (pinkie) of her left hand, in addition to multiple lacerations to the ankle, left leg, and left shoulder. The belayer suffered no injuries. Both climbers were wearing helmets.

None of the wounds was critical, and the injured climber was able to complete the pitch. The second climber then led the few remaining pitches to the top. They self-evacuated down to Contact Pass with the assistance of two other climbers, and eventually made it back to Second Lake and the trailhead. (*Source: Anonymous report from the belayer.*)

ANALYSIS

This is our second report in two years of a loose hold leading to injury on Temple Crag. The loose rock on this route and others on Temple Crag is frequently mentioned in trip reports and route descriptions. The leader did not test the quality of rock before placing full weight upon it, thus resulting in the fall and injury. Knocking on suspicious rock with the knuckles or palm can often reveal loose holds, which may be avoided. Additionally, the leader should have placed more protection to prevent such a long fall. Even though the climbing was easy for her (both climbers lead 5.10), it's important to place protection regularly on moderate terrain, especially when the rock quality is poor. (*Source: The Editors.*)

MT. WHITNEY AND PALISADES FATALITIES, SPLIT MOUNTAIN ACCIDENT: *Two climbers died in long falls on Mt. Whitney's upper slopes, on or near the Mountaineers Route, one in July and one in November. In June, a 67-year-old climber died in a long fall during his descent from the U-Notch after climbing North Palisade. Detailed reports were not available.*

A new report about a 2015 accident and rescue on Split Mountain, another California 14er, can be found by searching "Split Mountain inadequate belay" at publications.americanalpineclub.org.

FATAL FALLS ON UNUSUALLY ICY PEAK
Angeles National Forest, Mt. San Antonio (a.k.a. Mt. Baldy)

In February, three people plunged to their deaths down icy chutes on Mt. San Antonio (a.k.a. Mt. Baldy) or nearby; two of these were attempting to hike to the top of the 10,069-foot mountain on the Devil's Backbone Trail; a third person slipped and fell from nearby Icehouse Saddle. Mt. Baldy is the third-highest mountain in Southern California.

On February 2, Daniel Nguyen (23) slipped on ice and slid 1,500 feet to his death from the Devil's Backbone. The following Saturday, February 6, saw no easing of unusually icy conditions, and a dozen people had to be airlifted off Mt. Baldy as a result. One hiker, 47-year-old Dong Xing Liu, wasn't so lucky, as he died after slipping from Icehouse Saddle, located in a drainage southeast of Baldy. His wife also fell and suffered serious injuries to her lower body.

In the *Los Angeles Times*, on February 8, Mt. Baldy Fire Department Captain Gordon Greene described the icy conditions as "almost like a mirror," saying that even "crampons wouldn't have helped." Twelve days later, on February 20, a 45-year-old San Diego man who was wearing crampons plummeted 1,500 feet down a steep, icy chute on the north side of Mt.

The knife-edge ridge of the Devil's Backbone can become an icy technical climb in certain winter conditions. *Ben Baumann*

Harwood, directly east of Mt. Baldy on the Devil's Backbone ridge. The man's two companions, neither of whom were injured, also were wearing crampons.

Winter conditions on Mt. Baldy's upper reaches have taken the lives of other climbers, including Ali Aminian and Michelle Yu, both experienced mountaineers, in 2004 and 2010, respectively.

ANALYSIS

For much of the year, Mt. Baldy is a hiking destination for peak baggers, with the Devil's Backbone trail being the normal route. In places the spectacular ridge is only a few feet wide, with talus-filled gullies dropping away from either side of the ridge, but no technical climbing is involved. In certain winter conditions, however, crampons and ice axes may be necessary to negotiate the route, and mountaineering judgment—e.g., turning around in the face of severe conditions—is required. (*Source: Clay Jackson, with information from the Los Angeles Times.*)

JOSHUA TREE INCIDENT FEATURED ON THE SHARP END: *Individual accident reports from Joshua Tree National Park in 2016 were not received. However, a climber who had a serious downclimbing accident in November told his story in Episode 12 ("Shock in Joshua Tree") of the Sharp End podcast, produced by Ashley Saupe and the AAC.*

The northeast face of 14,259-foot Longs Peak in mid-May. Kiener's Route zigzags up snow ramps and ledges directly to the summit. *Frosty Weller*

COLORADO

STRANDED | Suspected Altitude Illness
Rocky Mountain National Park, Longs Peak

On Thursday, June 2, 10 soldiers from Fort Carson in Colorado Springs attempted to climb Kiener's Route on the northeast face of 14,259-foot Longs Peak. The soldiers, part of the 10th Special Forces Group, were engaged in a mountaineering exercise. Kiener's Route is a long snow and mixed climb, with the most difficult terrain above 13,000 feet, and generally has late-winter climbing conditions in early June.

The military group contacted park personnel when some of their party became "distressed," likely with altitude illness. They decided to spend an unplanned night at around 13,000 feet, and the following morning the stricken soldiers were helped to the summit by their team, where they were all evacuated by a civilian helicopter (contracted by the National Park Service) which made "seven or eight" trips to the top, according to ranger Mark Pita. More than 40 SAR personnel affiliated with the national park were on call to assist the soldiers to the summit if needed.

ANALYSIS

Acute mountain sickness (AMS) can strike nearly anyone who climbs too high too fast. Although it's not certain this is what "distressed" the stricken soldiers, they had rapidly reached a point about 7,000 feet higher than their base in Fort Carson. Normally, the definitive treatment for suspected altitude illness is to stop climbing or descend until symptoms resolve. However, the descent from this elevation on Kiener's Route can be chal-

SYMPTOMS OF AMS

Acute mountain sickness (AMS) may be present if a person who has climbed rapidly to a higher elevation develops a headache plus any of these symptoms:

- Gastrointestinal issues (nausea, vomiting, loss of appetite
- Fatigue/lassitude
- Dizziness/lightheadedness
- Insomnia or difficulty sleeping

lenging and time-consuming, and the team included trained medics who were able to provide treatment and observation. In consultation with rangers, they decided the soldiers were capable of continuing up the steep upper face to the flat summit, where a helicopter evacuation would be relatively easy to manage. (*Sources: Rocky Mountain National Park rangers, news reports, and the Editors.*)

FATAL GROUND FALL | Climbing Alone
Front Range, The Ironclads

On October 25, the body of 60-year-old Dr. James Lee "Jim" Detterline was found at the base of a small cliff in the Ironclads, a group of rock fins south of Rocky Mountain National Park. Detterline was a prominent figure in the national park, where he worked for more than two decades as Longs Peak supervisory climbing ranger, and where he was involved in hundreds of rescue missions. Known as "Mr. Longs Peak," he holds the record for most ascents (428) of the 14,259-foot mountain.

Detterline is known to have solo climbed at the Ironclads in the past, and his body was found with gear consistent with roped solo climbing. He died from internal injuries, likely due to a fall from one of the formations while attempting either to set up or remove a system for self-belayed climbing.

ANALYSIS
Jim Detterline was an extremely accomplished climber with decades of experience. His death illustrates the need for constant vigilance, even on familiar ground, and especially when scrambling unroped and/or climbing alone. When setting up a top-rope or other rope systems, constant edge awareness is essential. A temporary anchor often can be arranged to allow safe access to a cliff edge. (*Source: The Editors.*)

STRANDINGS IN THE FLATIRONS: *Rescuers were called several times in 2016 to help scramblers off the massive east-facing slabs of Boulder's Flatirons, where inexperienced climbers frequently are lured by easy access and gently angled climbing. One incident in August was notable because the scrambler spent the whole night on the face when he was unable to continue up or down; he said he was reluctant to call 911 out of concern he would be charged for the cost of a rescue. In the United States, search and rescue agencies almost never charge climbers for their services, though medical expenses, such as ambulance services, will be charged.*

LEADER FALL ONTO LEDGE | Protection Pulled Out
Eldorado Canyon, West Ridge

March 5 was a beautiful, sunny day in Eldo and I decided that after a good warmup I would put in a few burns on my project: Foxtrot (5.11d PG-13). I had top-roped this climb several times, doing it clean once.

I got up to the rest section just below a small roof and placed a yellow Metolius TCU (approximately 3/4-inch piece) in a seam. Above that piece is the crux of the route, and the next opportunity for gear is a tricky placement with a green Alien, followed by a seam higher up that takes small nuts. After a rest, I climbed up to the last move of the crux, a tricky layback or a long deadpoint to a positive flat edge.

I didn't have a green Alien (and I didn't know about that placement yet anyway), so I tried to deadpoint for the big edge but came up an inch short. The yellow TCU that I'd placed at the roof held my fall, which was clean and not too jarring.

I pulled up for another attempt and tried the same move with a little more umph but fell a second time. The piece held again. I looked over the placement and it seemed fine, so I decided to try again. I threw to the final hold and latched for a split second, cutting feet and swinging out from the wall Air Jordan–style. But then I slipped again and sailed through the air. This time the yellow TCU pulled out of the crack and I kept falling. My next piece was four to five feet below: an orange Metolius Master Cam placed in a good constriction. My fall extended another 10 feet or so. The rope began coming tight just as I got to the ledge that marks the start of the hard climbing, and I clipped the outside corner with my left foot before the rope stopped me a few feet later. I suffered an avulsion fracture on the medial malleolus and a fully torn superior peroneal retinaculum that required surgery to repair.

Making the crux move on Foxtrot. This climber is not related to the accident reported here. *Adam Brink*

ANALYSIS

The biggest mistake I made was not readjusting the cam into its ideal spot after taking the first fall. I just assumed that because the piece held a fall it must be solid. The crack is a bit shallow and downward-facing, since it is in a small roof, and the cam may have been sliding a small amount out of its ideal position in each fall, until it was close enough to the outside that it popped out.

The second big mistake I made was that I trusted just one piece of gear to catch my fall, and I didn't consider the consequences of the piece pulling out. Had I placed another piece adjacent to the one that pulled, or at least closer to my second-highest piece of pro, the ledge fall could have been prevented.

Finally, my familiarity with the route had led me to believe it was safe enough for me to project the climb on lead before I had every move and placement dialed. I obviously was not solid on the crux, and had I not fallen at all I would have been completely safe. My hard-man attitude about leading and taking falls got in the way of good risk assessment. (*Source: Mike Minson.*)

GROUND FALL IN ANTHILL DIRECT AREA: *A 24-year-old climber fell at least 70 feet to the ground at Redgarden Wall on April 9, sustaining significant injuries. The 5.8 variation he was attempting has a PG-13 hazard rating. A complete report was not available, but witnesses said the fall pulled out two of Black Diamond's smallest cams (the 0.1 and 0.2 Camalot X4, designed for aid climbing), the smaller of which was destroyed by the forces. A bolt that the climber had clipped low on the pitch may have slowed his fall somewhat before he impacted the ground. He was wearing a helmet and was expected to make a good recovery.*

ESSENTIALS

SHOCK
ASSESSMENT AND TREATMENT
By Dave Weber & Dr. Peter Hackett

Shock is inadequate delivery of oxygenated blood (perfusion) to the tissues and organs of the body. Insufficient perfusion results in deranged cell function initially and eventually cell death if left untreated. Climbers should be able to recognize the early signs of shock, assess its severity, and initiate treatment in order to maximize chances of recovery and prevent death. Documenting the signs of shock and changes in vital signs can provide critical information to first responders and medical caregivers.

Shock is a medical emergency, not to be confused with the term "shock" often incorrectly used to describe an acute stress response. In stressful scenarios, people may exhibit signs and symptoms that mimic the early stages of true shock but are transient and not a result of diminished perfusion. The short-lived effects of an acute stress response will usually last less than 15 minutes.

Causes of shock in the climbing and mountaineering environment can include severe dehydration from diarrhea, loss of blood from external or internal bleeding, impaired cardiac function, heart attack, severe allergic reaction, or spinal injury.

Shock is commonly classified in one of three categories: cardiogenic, hypovolemic, and vasogenic. These groupings correspond to the root cause of the shock physiology. Wilderness medicine educators often relate categories of shock to basic plumbing principles. Using this analogy, the complex physiology of shock can be simplified as problems originating with the pump (cardiogenic), not enough fluid (hypovolemic), or the pipes (vasogenic).

Cardiogenic shock is from the failure of the heart to pump blood effectively throughout the body. A heart attack causing poor pump function is an example of cardiogenic shock.

Hypovolemic shock results from low fluid volume within the system and is typically preventable with early recognition and management. Causes include fluid loss such as from bleeding, diarrhea, vomiting, or lack of oral fluid intake.

Vasogenic shock describes a loss of tone in the blood vessels (pipes) and thus increased space and decreased pressure within the system. This type of shock can be caused by a spinal cord injury, severe allergic reaction (anaphylaxis), or a system-wide infection (sepsis).

RECOGNITION AND ASSESSMENT

Recognizing shock requires the identification of likely causes and changes in vital signs characteristic of this condition. Assessment is based on trending of vital signs and symptoms, and can be divided into early and late stages. The following signs and symptoms describe the various stages of shock:

Early/Compensated Shock: The body struggles to maintain adequate circulation and blood pressure in response to reduced perfusion. Compensatory mechanisms include increased heart rate, increased respiratory rate, and constriction of blood vessels, especially in the skin. The patient's mental status may be anxious and restless. The skin may be pale, cool, and clammy (moist). A stable radial (wrist) pulse is present.

Late/Decompensated Shock: As compensation mechanisms begin to fail, inadequate perfusion detrimentally affects critical organs such as the brain. The patient may show disorientation, decreased alertness, and drowsiness. The skin is increasingly pale, cool, and clammy. Radial pulse weakens.

Late/Irreversible Shock: Cell and organ death result from continued lack of perfusion. The patient is unresponsive. The skin is cyanotic (blue) or ashen (gray). Radial pulse disappears.

FIELD TREATMENT

Shock is a medical emergency and wilderness treatment should focus on patient assessment, stabilization, and evacuation to definitive medical care.

- Treat the underlying cause.
  - Cardiogenic: Basic life support including airway management and cardiopulmonary resuscitation (CPR).
  - Hypovolemic: Control bleeding. Consider oral fluid replacement in any shock patient with normal mental status and the ability to swallow. Replace fluids orally at a maximum rate of one liter per hour.
  - Vasogenic: Treatments for shock of vasogenic origin are typically advanced and require evacuation to definitive medical care. Specific initial response to spinal cord injuries, anaphylaxis, and sepsis include spinal immobilization/restriction, administration of epinephrine, and an antibiotic regimen, respectively.
- Lay the patient flat.
- Consider elevating his or her legs.
- Keep the patient warm.
- Monitor vital signs every 5–15 minutes.
- If available, consider invasive fluid replacement (intravenous or intraosseous) and oxygen therapy.
- Evacuate any shock patient whose condition does not improve.

ADVANCED TREATMENT

Mild hypovolemic shock is usually the sole cause of this physiology that can be completely managed in the field. Advanced treatments for shock necessitate pre-hospital (ambulance) or hospital settings. Ultimately, prompt recognition, stabilization, documentation, and evacuation to definitive medical care are the most effective field treatments for the majority of these medical emergencies.

Note: The online version of this story (publications.americanalpineclub.org) includes a list of additional resources outlining the assessment and treatment of shock.

Dave Weber is a Denali mountaineering ranger and a flight paramedic for Intermountain Life Flight in Salt Lake City. Dr. Peter Hackett is a professor of emergency medicine at University of Colorado and director of the Institute for Altitude Medicine in Telluride, Colorado.

'TAKE' LEADS TO TWO CAMS PULLING OUT
Eldorado Canyon, West Ridge

On April 3, a 23-year-old female climber was climbing Sooberb (5.10c). Nearing the crux, a significant overhang split by a hand crack, the climber placed two pieces, one of which was a cam with only two lobes engaged. Fearing she might pump out on the crux above, she decided to rest by hanging from the rope clipped to the higher of the two cams, which looked more solid. That piece pulled out, as did the one below, and the climber fell 20 to 25 feet and sustained an ankle injury. Rocky Mountain Rescue Group performed the difficult technical rescue, which involved 25 people, several lowers, a long scree descent, and a river crossing.

ANALYSIS
Resting by hanging from traditional (removable) protection is not the same as clipping the rope to a quickdraw on a bolt and yelling "take!" When placing your own gear, you must be very sure a piece is solid before weighting it. If the pump clock is ticking, don't clip a suspect piece with your rope (which adds extra slack if the piece fails), but instead downclimb to a lower placement or stance. If you must rest on a suspect piece, clip into it directly instead of using the rope. This is also a good reminder to place gear frequently before a crux, even if the terrain is relatively easy. (*Sources: Eldorado Canyon State Park, Drew Hildner of Rocky Mountain Rescue Group, and the Editors.*)

GROUND FALL BEFORE REACHING FIRST PIECE
Eldorado Canyon, Roof Routes

Kurt Ross was belaying me (an experienced climber) on Guenese, a 5.11a trad route with a few fixed pieces. I considered placing a 0.5 Camalot in an overlap before clipping a piton, the first fixed pro on the route, but I didn't. I'm only 5 feet tall, and the pin felt very far away. I backed down once or twice before working out the right sequence for a shorter person. As I made the stand-up move to the piton, I popped off the wall and struck the ramp below, having fallen 10 to 15 feet. Kurt rushed over and asked me not to move, for fear of spinal injury. Luckily, there was none. I suffered a stress fracture of the cuboid (a small tarsal bone on the outer aspect of the foot), and I know I was lucky to have sustained only one injury.

ANALYSIS
Kurt had offered to clip the first piton for me, which, had I not been so prideful, could have saved me from a ground fall. He stands 6-feet, 4-inches, and would have no problem reaching the pin. In addition, I absolutely should have placed that Camalot before the pin. Perhaps pride clouded my judgment there as well. (*Source: Kathy Karlo.*) *Editor's note: Stick clips are rarely used in Eldorado Canyon, but they might prevent injuries like this. That said, fixed pitons should always be regarded with suspicion and should be backed up.*

INADEQUATE PLANNING FOR DESCENTS LEADS TO SERIOUS INJURIES: *In separate incidents, climbers in Clear Creek Canyon and Staunton State Park experienced ground falls as they were attempting to descend from single-pitch climbs. Only incomplete, third-person summaries of these accidents were available, but both* stemmed from inadequate preparation for descents from fixed anchors. The Clear Creek case involved miscommunication between the belayer and the climber, leading to a ground fall from an anchor atop a 5.9 sport climb. The other originated when an attempt to descend from a 170-foot 5.7 traditional pitch with a single rope came up short; after a second climber had scrambled up to a ledge to assist the stranded leader, she fell while attempting to return to the ground.

LEADER FALL | Rope Behind Leg
Garden of the Gods, Red Twin Spire

My climbing partner, Warren (23), and I (28) had come to Garden of the Gods during a climbing and hiking trip to Colorado from our home in Kentucky. It was almost 8:30 p.m. on July 23 by the time we finished hiking around the park, but we felt there was still enough time to sneak in a quick climb. One route seemed within our abilities: Potholes, a 5.7 route on a 60-foot sandstone spire, protected by two bolts and three pitons. We figured we'd make a quick climb of it before dark.

The route was casual, so it barely registered when I fell, about a foot below the fourth bolt. One second I was climbing and the next I was hanging upside down. Warren yelled out, "Are you good?" I replied, "Yeah, I'm good," but as I adjusted myself, I saw that my foot was pushed sideways. As I was falling, my right foot had caught behind the rope, shifting my weight so that my left foot hit the wall hard as I was inverting. Warren lowered me to the ground. Thanks to spectators below the climb, an ambulance was on the site within 30 minutes, and paramedics swiftly treated my dislocated ankle.

ANALYSIS

One of the bystanders caught my fall on video, and I have watched it dozens of times. (The video was highlighted as a *Rock and Ice* Weekend Whipper.) One of the major contributions to the injury was inadequate body awareness during the fall. Watching the video, I could see my body slide stiffly down the wall. Keeping my arms and legs relaxed and bent, out of the rope's way and ready to absorb impact, might have prevented the injury. Taking some controlled practice falls might ingrain better muscle memory for safer falls.

Although I did not sustain a head injury, I should have been wearing a helmet. Since I flipped over, my head traveled about 15 feet from its high point to low point. If the piton that caught me had pulled out, I would have fallen an additional 10 feet. In hindsight, it would have been smart to bring supplemental protection. (*Source: Philip Rodriguez.*)

GLISSADING WITHOUT ICE AXES
Sangre de Cristo Mountains, Humboldt Peak

On May 26, two climbers took long falls and sustained injuries while descending from 14,064-foot Humboldt Peak. Starting in midmorning from a campsite at the trailhead, they had snowshoed to the upper mountain and then climbed the easy west ridge, reaching the summit at 6 p.m.

To save time on the descent, they decided to glissade a snow gully on the southeast side, a quicker route back to the trail. They attempted to use their boots and trekking poles to control the speed. About halfway down, the snow hardened or turned to ice and both climbers lost control of their glissade, sliding several hundred feet before coming to a stop. Both had injuries, including a torn rotator cuff, broken arm, bruised ribs, a mild concussion, cuts, and abrasions.

One of the climbers used her cell phone to call for help at around 7:20 p.m. Both climbers were able to walk, and they said they would continue down along safer terrain while a team from Custer County Search and Rescue headed up the trail. By midnight they had descended into the trees at around 10,200 feet, stopped to rest, and built a fire. Here, rescuers found them and led them to the trailhead.

ANALYSIS
Although Humboldt is one of the easier 14ers in summer, the late-winter conditions of May make any peak of this size a more serious proposition. In a detailed description of the incident at her blog, one of the climbers cited numerous "lessons learned," including their failure to stick to a turnaround time or carry an adequate emergency kit. Fundamentally, however, this accident resulted from the decision to glissade unknown terrain without an ice axe. (*Source: Turnthepayge.com.*)

FATALITY ON CRESTONE NEEDLE: *An experienced 55-year-old mountaineer died in a 100-foot fall from 14,197-foot Crestone Needle in the Sangre de Cristos on July 9. Although he had climbed the peak at least twice, he and his team got off route and into more difficult terrain during their descent. Later the same month, Custer County SAR rescued another climbing team from nearly the same spot. On its website, the SAR team noted, "Despite trailhead kiosks warning of the dangers of descending off route, popular forums such as 14ers.com, and modern navigation tools, SAR teams continue to see climbers encounter difficulty and even death when descending off route, when they choose to continue to descend rather than...climbing back up to find the [correct route]."*

RAPPEL ERROR | Inadequate Anchor Knot
Raggeds Wilderness, Dark Canyon

In early January, two Colorado ice climbers began their third first ascent of the day in the Dark Canyon, 25 miles south of Redstone in the Raggeds Wilderness. Duane Raleigh (age 56, with 43 years of experience) was leading the first pitch of the WI3+ M4 route. Due to thin ice, the only protection he placed on the 230-foot pitch was a stubby screw at approximately 75 feet. Raleigh reached the end of the rope without finding an anchor, so he asked his partner (40 years of experience) to take him off belay, so he could continue climbing and searching for an anchor.

Raleigh spotted a precarious stack of granite that he thought might be secure enough to sling for a rappel anchor. He tested the pile by hitting it with a tool and then pulling on it. Although apprehensive about the anchor's stability, he had no better option, so he wrapped a 10-foot 6mm cord around the rocks and tied the ends together with a flat figure-8 knot, visually checking and tugging the knot to test it. He then clipped his rope to the cord with a carabiner, planning to downclimb most of the route to minimize weighting the anchor.

Due to the steepness of the first 10 feet of this descent, Raleigh leaned back and

[Left] **The flat overhand is a proven knot for joining rappel ropes when properly tied and tightened, with 15- to 18-inch-long tails.** [Right] **The flat figure-8 should not be used.**

weighted the rope. He ended up in a free fall and landed 15 feet below, upside down, in a small patch of soft snow in a dihedral. He was uninjured except for two crampon punctures in his thigh. Raleigh climbed back up, expecting that the anchor rocks had failed. Instead, he found an untied 6mm cord. He retied the cord with a retraced figure-8 bend (Flemish bend) and successfully downclimbed and lowered to the good screw he'd placed at 75 feet. He pulled the rope and then lowered to the ground from the screw. (*Sources: Rock and Ice magazine and Duane Raleigh.*)

ANALYSIS

Although not verifiable by the climber, it is possible that the flat figure-8 may have capsized under load, flipping and rolling down the cord until the knot reached the ends of the cord and untied. Both the flat figure-8 and the flat overhand knot have been used to join two rappel ropes, and both can capsize under heavy loads. However, a well-tied flat overhand is much less likely to do so and is strongly recommended over the flat figure-8, which accounts for most reported failures of this general category of rappel knot.

When tying the flat overhand to join two rappel ropes, always tie a well-dressed knot and leave long tails (15 to 18 inches). Individually tighten all four strands of rope entering the knot. If using ropes of different diameters, age, or condition, or icy or wet ropes, consider tying a second overhand immediately adjacent to the first as a backup, though this will increase the bulk of the knot. Or, if there are no concerns about the knot snagging when the rappel ropes are pulled, consider the double fisherman's knot or Flemish bend, which are very reliable, albeit more difficult to untie after loading.

Do not use the flat overhand to join ropes permanently (e.g., tying a cordelette or tying a rope around a tree for an anchor). The double fisherman's knot is preferred for these purposes. Also, do not use the flat overhand for tying slings or webbing. Use a water knot for slings that may be retied and a double fisherman's for permanent knots. Again, dress all knots carefully and tighten every strand. (*Sources: Rock and Ice magazine and the Editors.*)

LEADER FALL ON ICE | Hit by Unknown Falling Object
Ouray, Camp Bird Road

On January 5, Dale Remsberg (44), an IFMGA guide and very experienced ice climber, was teaching an AMGA I2 Ice Instructor Course to students Aili Farquhar, the belayer at time of accident, and Kerr Adams. While leading pitch two of the Skylight (WI4+), midway up the pitch, Remsberg stopped to place his third ice screw, about 10 feet above his previous screw. During this process, he coached the students and described why he was placing another screw relatively soon (the previous placement had hit some air pockets and produced some surface cracking). Before he completed the third screw, Remsberg was hit by an unknown falling object, possibly a snow mushroom. The belay stance for this pitch is down a snow slope and around a corner, making it difficult to maintain a belay with minimal slack. The resulting fall was around 35 feet down an ice chimney. Remsberg's second ice screw held, and the belay halted the fall just before he hit an ice ledge at the start of the pitch.

"SOAP notes" were compiled on the climber's status while responders waited for an ambulance to arrive.

With Remsberg still conscious, the well-trained students were able to self-rescue via a lower and then tandem rappel to the road below the climb. Meanwhile, at the top of pitch one, Adams had called 911 and Remsberg called Nate Disser, the owner of San Juan Mountain Guides (SJMG). When guides from SJMG arrived on the scene, they aided Farquhar in conducting a thorough head-to-toe assessment and vitals check and produced SOAP (Subjective, Objective, Assessment, Plan) notes that were used during transport to a trauma center. An ambulance carried Remsberg to Ouray, from which he was flown via helicopter to the hospital in Montrose. He suffered three fractured ribs and a hemopneumothorax (abnormal air and blood in the chest cavity).

ANALYSIS

Dale Remsberg writes: I do not believe really anything went wrong in this incident, but rather everything went as well as it could. I had subscribed to the "ice leader must never fall" philosophy for 25 years and had never taken a leader fall on ice before. This climb was well within my ability and was in good shape. My takeaway was that, even when everything is done as well as possible, unfortunate things can happen and it's very important to have partners that have practiced self-rescue and have first-aid knowledge.

In addition, the fact that we had cell phone coverage made a huge difference in response time. Climbers should consider other forms of communication if they go out of cell range. I carry a two-way satellite communication device and a satellite phone on remote climbs. The trauma surgeon stated that if I not been able to get to definitive care as soon as I had, the outcome likely would have been much worse. (*Source: Dale Remsberg.*)

LINCOLN FALLS NEAR MISS: *An experienced ice climber had a very close call in the Mosquito Range in February when a large sheet of ice (estimated at 10 by 6 feet) broke loose under him while he was leading the popular Scottish Gully (WI3). He fell about 40 feet into snow near the base of the climb. Prudently, he'd placed a screw partway up and the rope came tight as he neared the ground, preventing an even longer fall—a good reminder to place adequate protection even on relatively easy climbs.*

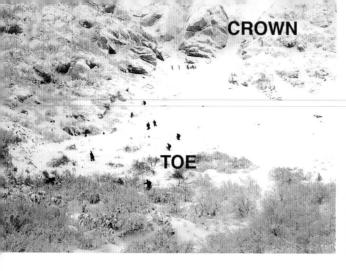

CROWN

TOE

Rescuers probe the debris of an avalanche in Tuckerman Ravine that caught five people in its path. *Mount Washington Avalanche Center*

NEW HAMPSHIRE

AVALANCHE

Mt. Washington, Tuckerman Ravine

Two climbers and three skiers were involved in an avalanche in Tuckerman Ravine on Sunday, January 17. The two climbers, both from Canada, were ascending a gully called the Chute on the left side of the ravine. Four skiers and an avalanche class were nearby at the time. Just before 1 p.m., the pair climbed over an old fracture line, a foot to a foot and a half high, and continued into softer snow. After ascending approximately 30 feet through deeper snow, the climber in front felt that the slope might be unstable and decided to turn around. As they turned to descend, the slope fractured about 75 to 100 feet above them and approximately 75 to 100 feet wide. The two climbers were carried most of the distance to the ravine floor. Three nearby skiers also were caught and carried varying distances by the debris.

One of the two climbers sustained non-life-threatening injuries and was treated and released by snow ranger staff and the Mt. Washington Volunteer Ski Patrol. One of the skiers also received non-life-threatening injuries.

ANALYSIS

The Mt. Washington Observatory reported 5.5 inches of snow on the summit during the previous day, with around four inches falling at Hermit Lake at the base of Tuckerman Ravine. Summit winds blew 40–60 mph overnight from the west. The wind diminished to 20 mph as visitors began to enter Tuckerman. An avalanche bulletin posted on Saturday morning had accurately described recent and upcoming snowfall and wind loading in the area.

Although everyone involved in this incident was appropriately clothed for winter conditions and some of the individuals were equipped and trained to apply first aid to the injured, none of the five people caught in the avalanche was wearing beacons or carrying avalanche rescue gear. Sadly, this is not unusual in our terrain. Frequently, climbers leave behind avalanche rescue gear to save weight, leaving no quick course of action should burial occur.

Given the clustering of users near the Chute, it seems safe to assume that the "social proof" heuristic was at play. Following some discussion, the avalanche class chose to travel in steep terrain beneath a recently loaded slope. They were followed by the party of two climbers and the three skiers. Whether due to the easier travel following in someone else's boot track, the erroneous assumption that a slope is safe because someone else already has traveled it, or the belief that other travelers know more than you, this behavior is all too common in Tuckerman Ravine.

Additional challenges exist when trying to rebalance risk on a continual basis, based on the actions of others outside your control. Mt. Washington has very concentrated avalanche terrain and a high amount of visitation. Your party's movements may be under tight control and stay within your chosen level of accepted risk, but only in the absence of other, more unpredictable people. An associated concern is the challenge of spreading out to reduce overall risk in a relatively confined area.

The two climbers overlooked a red flag when they climbed over a recently reloaded crown line and onto a slope that rises from 40° to 45° or more. Moreover, all parties involved in the Chute incident crossed beneath this slope within four hours of a period of active loading. While everyone chooses their own level of acceptable risk, it is unclear whether all parties involved had sought the information needed to make an informed decision by reading the posted General Avalanche Bulletin or seeking recent weather data. (*Source: Mount Washington Avalanche Center.*)

SLIDING FALL BEFORE ROPING UP
Mt. Washington, Huntington Ravine

At approximately 12:10 p.m. on Sunday, February 7, one member of a climbing party of three slipped while approaching a technical snow and ice climb in Huntington Ravine. The climber rapidly gained speed on the 35–40° snow slope beneath Central Gully and tumbled into the rocks below, sustaining non-life-threatening injuries.

As many parties do, this group planned to rope up at a terrain bench beneath the ice bulge marking the start of the steepest climbing in Central Gully. The most experienced climber went first and coached the two less experienced climbers to use both tools to climb 10 feet of exposed ice in order to reach the flat platform. The second and least experienced of the three slipped while climbing this section. After losing both ice tools, the climber managed to orient her feet downhill but soon caught a crampon in the snow. Starting to tumble, she came to a stop after falling approximately 200 feet, sustaining ankle and shoulder injuries.

ANALYSIS
Long, sliding falls are the leading cause of injuries in Tuckerman and Huntington ravines. Four days prior to this incident, temperatures on the mountain soared into the mid-30s (F) for over 24 hours. Following this, the temperature dropped to near 0°F. These conditions created a very hard and icy snowpack. Melt-freeze crusts can often make self-arresting impossible.

It is important to assess snow conditions and combine this with an honest assessment of the experience of members of a party. Depending on the competence and risk tolerance of party members, even low-angle snow slopes may need to be belayed in order to assure safe passage. The conditions this day were far from ideal and required a greater measure of security for a team that included novice alpine climbers. (*Source: Mount Washington Avalanche Center.*)

MORE FALLS ON MT. WASHINGTON: *On March 13, two long, sliding falls caused serious injuries on Mt. Washington. In the first, a skier fell about 1,000 feet in Hill-man's Highway and hit several rocks during his slide, requiring a helicopter evacuation. Soon afterward, a hiker on the summit cone fell and broke his femur while glissading terrain the party had not ascended. That weekend, icy conditions had been caused by warm, rainy weather followed by a hard freeze. In-depth accounts and analyses of these incidents and others may be found at mountwashingto-navalanchecenter.org.*

BENIGHTED AND STRANDED
White Mountain National Forest, Cannon Cliff

On November 19, two men in their 20s started up a long climb in the Vertigo area. The pair had a single rope and adequate clothing for a full day out. After the first four or five pitches of most routes in this area of Cannon, the climbing tends to peter into brushy ledges punctuated by short slabs, and route-finding can become difficult. By nighttime the pair was still climbing. Both climbers felt that retreat wasn't an option. Late at night, about 200 feet from the top of the cliff, the climbers called Fish and Game to request a rescue. Six members of Mountain Rescue Service hiked up the backside of Cannon and set up a haul system, which they used to pull up the stranded climbers. They all reached the road by midmorning.

ANALYSIS
This scenario is not uncommon on Cannon. The upper sections of the cliff are loose and route-finding is difficult. Carrying a tagline to expedite retreats is a good idea, but it's also possible to rappel the first half of many routes with a single 70-meter rope—most pitches are short, having been climbed mainly in the 1970s, and many safe fixed anchors exist. By the time the rescue team arrived, rain and high wind had moved in. In late November, with short days and very cold nights, good judgment becomes even more important on long routes like this. Bailing off a climb can be more daunting than finishing, but keeping this avenue open is an important part of any climbing day. (*Source Michael Wejchert, Mountain Rescue Service.*)

BROKEN HOLD | Inadequate Protection
North Conway, Humphrey's Ledge

On May 28, a party was climbing at Humphrey's Ledge, just outside of North Conway. The leader was attempting a climb called Sting Like a Butterfly, an obscure 5.10. A handhold broke as the climber was pulling through the crux of the route and the climber fell. As he did, a cam he'd placed in a loose flake pulled loose. The climber hit the slab below, breaking his femur. A team from the Mountain Rescue Service was mobilized, and they lowered the injured climber in a rescue litter after stabilizing him.

ANALYSIS

Humphrey's Ledge is notorious for sections of rotten rock. While breaking a handhold could happen at any crag, special care must be taken when attempting a climb at or close to one's limit on bad rock or on routes that do not see frequent traffic. Testing holds, taking care to place protection in the most solid rock available, and never climbing too far above marginal gear are all part of a larger contingency plan, but perhaps most important is staying in control to avoid a fall that might result in injury—including downclimbing when necessary. (*Source Michael Wejchert, Mountain Rescue Service.*)

LONG LEADER FALL
North Conway, Cathedral Ledge

On July 31, Stephanie Angione was leading the second pitch of Still in Saigon, a popular 5.8 at Cathedral Ledge, when she fell at the crux, sailed past her gear, and broke her foot upon impacting the rock. The crux is protected by a good horizontal cam placement and, a body length higher, a bolt. Her belayer lowered her all the way to the ground, and two climbers who were nearby carried Angione back to the road.

ANALYSIS

Lower-angle climbs often have worse injury potential than steeper, more difficult ones; an abundance of ledges contributes to this hazard. That said, the crux of Still in Saigon is reasonably well protected, and a fall normally should not result in injury. The length of this fall suggests the climber either had pulled up a lot of slack to clip the bolt or the belayer had too much slack in the system. (The rescuers who responded believed the latter was the case.) Either way, this is an opportunity to remind readers that the practice of belaying with some slack in the rope in hopes of offering a "soft catch," usually learned in sport climbing settings, is inappropriate on many lower-angle climbs, where protecting against a fall onto ledges or other features is the top priority. (*Source Michael Wejchert, Mountain Rescue Service.*)

LOWERING ERROR | Rope Too Short For Climb
Rumney, Parking Lot Wall

On September 8, two men were climbing Shealyn's Way (5.7), a sport route approximately 75 feet high. As the leader was lowering from the top, approximately 25 to 30 feet from the ground, the tail of the rope passed through the belayer's device and the climber fell to the ground, sustaining an injury to his lower extremities.

ANALYSIS

These climbers were using a 40-meter rope—much too short for a climb this long. The rope had been cut to a length suitable for gym climbing but not for most outdoor use. A stopper knot in the end of the rope (or tying in the belayer) would have prevented this accident, despite the inappropriate rope. In addition, neither climber was wearing a helmet. The chance of head trauma in this case was very high, as the climber fell right between two rocks. (*Source: Grant Farmer.*)

NEW MEXICO

LEADER FALL | Inexperience, Inadequate Protection
Sandia Mountains, Muralla Grande

On August 14, a leader (male, 40s) was attempting the third pitch of La Selva (5.8), which begins in low fifth-class terrain and steepens into a dihedral with a wide crack before an exit left on vertical terrain. The leader placed a number 4 Camalot for his last piece of protection. He was five or six feet above this Camalot when he came off, falling approximately 15 feet and landing on a ledge and striking his right hip. There was 150 to 170 feet of rope in service at the time of the fall.

The climber was able to stand up and secure an anchor in order to bring up the second. However, every time he internally or externally rotated his right hip, he

experienced moderate pain in the joint. Fearing that he may have had a pelvic fracture, the party initiated a rescue by calling 911.

As is usual for high-angle rescues in New Mexico, a multi-agency effort was required. The second climber was extricated first, because the injured subject was stable and potential rockfall from a litter evacuation would pose a great hazard to the uninjured climber and anyone else at the belay ledge below. The injured climber was then secured with a pelvic splint and Stokes litter, and a 450-foot raise was performed to the top of Muralla Grande. It was reported that the leader suffered a minor nondisplaced pelvic fracture.

ANALYSIS

Crux passages of climbs, especially those with low-angle terrain or ledges immediately below the crux, mandate extra care and protection. The description of this pitch at Mountain Project suggests that "leaders at their limit may want a second large cam" for the wide crack. Some climbers break this rope-stretching pitch in two, which puts the belayer closer to the crux, greatly reducing rope stretch and improving the belayer's ability to react to a

Rescuers accompany a litter during a 450-foot raise to the top of Muralla Grande in the Sandias. James Marc Beverly

fall. Guides often use shorter pitches to improve communication and safety without hindering speed. (*Sources: James Marc Beverly and Erin Renee Beverly.*)

LOWERING ERROR | Clipped Wrong Rope Into Anchor
Diablo Canyon, Sun Devil Wall

On January 18, at approximately 2 p.m., Climber 1 fell from the top anchors of pitch two of Appendicitis (5.10a) on the Sun Devil Wall. She fell approximately 170 feet to the ground. Trained medical professionals were climbing nearby and immediately rendered aid, including CPR. An emergency medical helicopter was quickly called

ESSENTIALS

CLEAR WEIGHT TRANSITIONS
A CRITICAL YET OFTEN IGNORED STEP

By Molly Loomis

Cochise Stronghold, Arizona: A climbing instructor stands on a ledge, cleaning an anchor for her students. Amid multiple pieces of tat, she incorrectly threads the rope on which she is to be lowered. She misses the error due to excess slack in the system. She leans back to be lowered and falls.

Kelso, Ontario: A climber leans back to initiate a rappel. Only one strand of the rappel rope is clipped through his descent device. He falls.

High Sierra, California: A climber cleans an anchor and calls to be lowered. Her partner misunderstands and takes her off belay. The climber falls.

What do all three of these real-world incidents have in common, aside from tragic injury and death? In each case, the accident *might* have been avoided by a climber consciously making a clear weight transition from one piece of cord, rope, or webbing to another. Partner checks and clear communication can help avoid such accidents, but ultimately it's up to each climber to perfect such transitions.

At hanging belays or rappel stations without any big ledges to stand on, gravity makes it relatively easy to see which rope or sling is holding the climber's weight. Whether you're clipping into an anchor after climbing, rigging for a rappel, or getting ready to be lowered, the question of which piece of material is holding your weight is quickly answered in a tangible, tactile fashion.

But at belay stances where you can stand up and unweight your harness, transitions can be murkier and extra vigilance is required. Likewise, familiar climbs and/ or climbing partners we've known for decades can breed transition complacency. In all cases, it's essential to verify that you've moved correctly from one anchor or belay system to the next *before* you unclip from the previous one.

The most common failures to make clear weight transitions occur when moving from an anchor to a rappel or lower. But the same thinking applies to all sorts of climbing transitions: switching the follower from a top belay onto the anchor; switching from giving a lead belay to receiving a top belay; or a leader transitioning off an anchor tether into leading. In short, clear transitions are important every time you're switching from relying on one particular rope, cord, or piece of webbing to another.

Here's a walk-through showing one example of a clear weight transition at a rappel station. Imagine you're standing on ledge with an anchor at chest height. You have already tethered into the rappel anchor and threaded the rope for descent. Now:

(1) Double-check your attachments to the anchor, then consciously transition your weight as much as possible onto your tether(s) or personal anchor sys-

tem. Step down or lean back so you are fully hanging in your harness from your tether (or tethers).* This clearly demonstrates which pieces of cordage are taking full weight.

(2) Grab the rope strands and rig your rappel device and your third-hand backup.

(3) Stand up tall to pull as much rope slack through your rappel device as possible. Repeat until *all* your weight has been transferred onto the rappel ropes and there is just enough slack in your tethers that you will be able to unclip them. Here is where you get irrefutable, tangible proof that your body weight has been fully transferred from your tethers to your rappel lines—otherwise your attachments to the anchor would still be weighted.

(4) Engage your brake hand and unclip your tethers.

A clear weight transition is easily achieved at a hanging stance. After setting up the rappel or threading the rope to lower, pull up and lock off the rappel ropes or ask your belayer to "take" so that all of your weight is on the new system. Now there should be some slack in your anchor tethers, clearly verifying that your weight is safely being held by the new system before you unclip your tethers. *Rick Weber*

Of course, you may encounter situations where performing a clear weight transition is more difficult: when your rappel device is extended from your belay loop with a long sling, for example, or when rappel anchors are situated below waist level, such as slings around the base of a tree. In such cases, the goals of clear transitions still apply, and the deviation from your usual habit should prompt heightened awareness and an extra run-through of your mental checklist for the transition. Even if you cannot follow the exact steps outlined above, you can and should always weight-test the new system before unclipping from the anchor.

It takes just a few seconds to make this safety check—seconds that could mean the difference between a fun outing and a funeral.

Molly Loomis has worked as a guide, outdoor educator, and climbing ranger. She and Andy Tyson co-authored Climbing Self Rescue: Improvising Solutions for Serious Situations.

---

* I like Purcell prusiks as anchor tethers because they offer a smooth, efficient way to transition weight even while the tether is loaded.

and arrived within one hour. The climber died at the scene from her injuries without regaining consciousness.

ANALYSIS

Diablo Canyon, near Santa Fe, has multiple routes longer than 30 to 35 meters, and parties will frequently set up a long top-rope, using two ropes tied together, for others to climb the route after one climber has led it. On the day of this accident, others in this climbing party (Climber 2, Climber 3) led the route in two pitches and then set up a two-rope system, using two slings and four locking carabiners at the top anchor. The two ropes were of similar diameter and ample length, and were joined with a triple fisherman's knot. Climber 2 and Climber 3 then rappelled the route in one double-rope rap.

The climbing party's procedure for top-roping on two ropes involved belaying on the side of the joined ropes with the fisherman's knot. In order to avoid the need to pass the fisherman's knot when it reached the belay device, the climber would tie in short on the other strand of rope, clipping a figure 8 on a bight to a locking carabiner clipped to the belay loop of his or her harness. Therefore, the climber had a long tail of extra rope dangling while climbing. This top-rope setup was common for the crag, and the climbing party was local. Others in the party top-roped the route in the same manner on that day without incident.

The next climber on the route (Climber 4) carried steel carabiners to leave as fixed gear at the anchors, attaching them to existing chains on the two anchor bolts to facilitate anchor cleaning and lowering. Many routes in the area have fixed carabiners for lowering, left by earlier climbers.

As the last person to top-rope the route for the day, Climber 1 agreed to clean the anchors. She planned to transfer the rope from the slings and lockers at the anchor to the two new fixed carabiners and remove all the other gear. Climber 1 then would be lowered, which was communicated to the belayer (Climber 4) before starting the climb.

Climber 1, age 59, had extensive personal experience with this method of top-roping and cleaning anchors. Her typical procedure would have been to (1) clip directly into both anchor bolts using a personal anchor system; (2) remove the temporary anchor attachments, letting the rope hang from her harness attachment point; (3) place the rope into the fixed carabiners for lowering; (4) check her setup; and (5) remove her personal anchor system to be lowered. On this occasion, Climber 1 called several times to the belayer for "take" and "slack," which was presumed to be verifying the rope arrangement. Then, presumably after removing her personal anchor system from the bolts, Climber 1 fell to the ground.

The most likely explanation is that Climber 1 confused which side of the rope running from the bight clipped to her belay loop was the end tied to the second rope; she apparently thought the free-hanging length of tail was the side being belayed and incorrectly clipped that side into the fixed carabiners. Thus, once she unclipped from the anchor bolts and weighted the rope, the free-hanging tail of rope quickly ran through the carabiners. After the fall, it was observed that the cleaned anchor attachments and Climber 1's personal anchor system were clipped to and intact on her harness, her harness had no damage, and her figure 8 knot was still tied correctly and attached to her harness via a bight with an undamaged locking carabiner. Both ropes were intact and fell to the ground with her, still tied together.

If the two ropes hanging from the figure 8 on a bight clipped to her harness had twisted and wrapped around each other, this might have led to confusion about the correct strand of the rope to clip into the steel carabiners for lowering, particularly since both strands would be the same color and pattern. The tail of the rope would have been at least 50 to 60 feet long (not an insignificant length or weight). If the personal anchor system clipped to the bolts was relatively short, her weight may have been held mostly by that system (almost a hanging belay), making the tug of "take" more subtle. The long distance of the two-pitch route made communication difficult, especially because a breeze was blowing. It was also the last climb of the day, and she may have been fatigued after climbing the full 170-foot route.

This accident has served as a sobering reminder to local climbers to take more time to double-check ourselves and our partners. Some climbers who top-rope these long routes at Diablo Canyon now place both strands of the rope that's clipped to their belay loop into the lowering carabiners at the anchors; this ensures that even if the trail rope accidentally is clipped, the main belay rope will be clipped too. Others are now in the habit of having the last person rappel to clean the route instead of lowering; we recognize that you still must not screw up the rappel, but there is less potential for confusion.

Climber 1 was a pillar of the local community, who introduced many people to climbing, and is terribly missed by all who knew her. (*Source: Heather Volz, in collaboration with the local climbing community.*)

NEW YORK

LEADER FALL ON ICE | Thin Ice, Inadequate Protection
Adirondacks, Pitchoff Mountain

My two partners and I (male, age 40), all experienced climbers, were in the Adirondacks on January 26 for the AAC Metro New York Section's Winter Outing. We decided to climb Screw and Climaxe, a well-known, 350-foot WI3+ on the north side of Pitchoff Mountain.

Screw and Climaxe is notoriously thin, particularly in the bottom section. From the base, the first pitch looked thin but climbable. I couldn't fully assess the thickness of the ice on the entire route because the wall was plastered with snow, but I could see plenty of ice near the top. Normally, I am very cautious and conservative, and I only lead if I can get good protection; I've retreated from several ice leads before. But the first part looked doable, so I decided to give it a try.

The thin first pitch led to a ledge about 75 feet up. The second pitch started with some low-angle sections with snow and ice accumulation, and I was able to put in a stubby ice screw. I headed for a shrub in a corner and found a frozen-in sling. I clipped that and backed it up with a poor nut in a shallow, icy crack. The next bit was a moderately angled slab covered in verglas. I placed a stubby screw partway into some softish ice, then spent some time trying different routes up the slab. There was a good belay stance at a tree about 15 feet up and far to the right. Above the tree, the ice appeared to be considerably more abundant. After considering my options, including retreat, I decided to climb toward the tree. I was about two-thirds of the way across the slab and 60 feet above the belay when I fell.

The top stubby screw and the worthless nut ripped out. My right leg hit the belay ledge, and I finally stopped falling about 15 feet from the base of the climb. The frozen sling on the shrub had held and kept me from hitting the ground.

The fall fractured my femur and patella, and cracked my sternum and skull. My partners called 911 and Department of Environmental Conservation (NYDEC) rangers responded quickly, reaching me two hours after the emergency call went out. Rescuers belayed a litter carrying me down talus to the pond at the base of Pitchoff, and then a sled pulled by a snowmobile brought me to a waiting ambulance.

The next day, when my partners and some friends went back to collect our gear, they estimated I had fallen 130 feet. I had surgery to place a rod and screws in my femur, and since then I have made a good recovery.

The WI3+ route Screw and Climaxe on Pitchoff Mountain often has very thin ice low on the climb. *R.L. Stolz/ verticalperspectivesphotography.com*

ANALYSIS

I should have chosen a different route with adequate ice, and I am now avoiding routes where I can't visually confirm the condition of the entire climb before starting up. When the route revealed itself to be in poor shape partway up, I should have retreated. I can't say precisely why I continued, except that I was motivated to finish so my partners could have a good day of climbing. Better communication with my partners would have helped. As it turns out, they had also been thinking that retreat would be the best option, given the conditions. If one of us had verbalized this suggestion, we probably all would have agreed to turn around. (*Source: Anonymous report from the leader.*)

FALL ON ICE | Using Microspikes Instead of Crampons
Adirondacks, Haystack Mountain

I organized a trip to the High Peaks region of the Adirondacks for March. The plan was to summit Mt. Haystack, Saddleback Mountain, and Basin Mountain in one day, under late-winter conditions, in order to simulate a long alpine climb. There were nine people in our party, mostly from the D.C. area, with varying degrees of experience. Although I had decades of backcountry travel under my belt, including eight years in the military, I was relatively new to mountaineering, but I had completed a winter ascent of Mt. Marcy, the highest peak in the Adirondacks, the previous year. As the trip leader (age 35), I had decided that we did not need ropes and harnesses, but I told each climber to bring the required winter gear, including snowshoes, crampons, and ice axe.

We planned to summit Mt. Haystack, eight miles from the trailhead, by way of Little Haystack, a subordinate peak just to the north. It was clear but cold (20°F) at the trailhead. We started off on snowshoes but switched to crampons where the trail to Little Haystack split off. Once we reached the summit of Little Haystack, we took a break to assess the route ahead: a steep and rocky descent into a col before a scramble up to Mt. Haystack's summit. Much of the rock was covered with ice, and three members of our party were uncomfortable with the conditions and turned back. Among the six of us who decided to press on was my younger brother, Chris, who was wearing Kahtoola Microspikes rather than crampons.

As we began the difficult descent of Little Haystack, we had not gone 50 feet when my brother, directly behind me, started sliding. I intentionally fell on top of him, hoping to stop his slide and arrest both of us with my ice axe and crampons. Instead, we both continued to slide. My brother was able to grab a rock to stop himself. Having lost my grip on my ice axe, I continued sliding until I forcefully planted my right crampon onto a rock outcropping. I stopped just a few feet short of a cliff.

When I rolled over, I saw that my right foot had flopped over, and trying to stand was very painful. We tried to call 911 but couldn't get a cell signal. Soon another hiker came along and pressed his SPOT emergency beacon. We waited in place for about two hours but gradually lost hope for a rescue and decided to start back toward the cars.

I spent the next two hours crawling back up Little Haystack and down to where we had stashed our snowshoes. I made a splint from one of my snowshoes, but it didn't help much. I soon tried my cell phone again and was able to get a signal. The 911 dispatcher knew who I was and advised that forest rangers and a state police helicopter were on their way. The rescue party reached me about 20 minutes later, packaged me in a litter, and lifted me to a hospital in Saranac Lake. My right fibula had fractured in two places, and my ankle was dislocated.

ANALYSIS

My brother's fall started the chain of events that ended with my injuries, and it probably could have been avoided if he been wearing crampons instead of Microspikes. I didn't know he was improperly equipped until we ditched our snowshoes. As trip leader, I should have done a gear check the night before, and I should have turned him around when it became apparent that Microspikes were inadequate for the conditions.

Furthermore, this was the first time some climbers in our party had ever held an ice axe, including my brother. I did not train anyone before the outing to self-arrest. Finally, if I had carried a SAM splint in my first-aid kit, I could have better splinted my leg, which would have made for a slightly more comfortable crawl up and down Little Haystack. (*Source: Shaun So.*)

GROUND FALL | Loose Rock, Inadequate Belay
Adirondacks, Starbuck Mountain

The following report is condensed from "Unbelayvable: A Missed Catch," published November 2016 in Climbing magazine, with permission of the author, Kevin Corrigan, and the climber, Annie Nelson.

I'm a 20-year-old from upstate New York. Last August I met a pair of climbers at Shelving Rock, and we made plans to check out a new wall called Starbuck Cliff.

One of the guys canceled last minute, so it was just me and his partner, who said he was an experienced climber. I'd just started leading trad in the spring, but was excited to try a crack climb that looked to be about 5.8, though we had no guidebook.

The bottom was casual. By the time I was 60 feet up, I had five solid pieces below me. My left hand was on a jug, and I was trying to decide what to place in the crack in front of me. Then the jug unexpectedly came out of the wall. Without thinking, I chucked it down in the direction of my belayer, yelling "Rock!"

My belayer, who was wearing a helmet, took a step backward and raised his hands in the air. The step back tugged at the rope against my harness. His instinct took over, and he let go of the rope to take another step back. I was trying to recover my balance, but the tug didn't help. I fell about 60 feet and hit the ground. My belayer, in his surprise, never recovered the rope. I landed flat on my back, on a small strip of soft dirt between two boulders.

The fall knocked me out, luckily erasing all memory of the event. When I woke, for a few seconds I couldn't see or breathe. It felt like there was an enormous weight on my chest. Slowly everything returned. I was incredibly sore, but nothing felt broken so I packed up my stuff, walked to my car, and drove to the ER. (I know I shouldn't have.) To the amazement of myself, my friends, and the doctors, all I suffered was some slightly cracked ribs and a mild head injury—not even a concussion. My helmet may have saved my life.

ANALYSIS

There are a few things we can all do to avoid such incidents:

- Assess the holds. Knock on the rock, does it sound hollow? Does it shift at all when you grab it? These are warning signs. (*Editor's note: If a hold comes off, be sure to throw it away from your belayer!*)
- Assess new partners. It's important to know the experience level of your climbing partner and plan accordingly. However, even an experienced climber may not react appropriately to a surprise situation like rockfall.
- Assess the belay area. Before climbing, identify where it will be safest to belay (or flee to) should rockfall occur.
- Consider an assisted-braking belay device. These devices add an extra measure of security if your belayer is incapacitated by rockfall or other events. (*Sources: Annie Nelson and Kevin Corrigan.*)

GROUND FALL | Small Cams Pulled Out
Adirondacks, Chapel Pond Pass

Our party of six, with three experienced climbers and three newbies, headed to the Lower Beer Walls on June 25. I chose to lead a 5.8 trad route, Rockaholic, a left-leaning finger crack on polished granite.

As I started up the climb, I placed a nut and then a micro-cam. My third placement was also a micro-cam, a 0.2 Black Diamond X4, in a flared crack. There was a better place in the crack for the cam, but I didn't want to block a good handhold. By this time I was about 40 feet off the ground and getting pumped out, so I quickly placed a 0.4 Black Diamond X4 and leaned back to rest on the rope. But the cam shifted as I weighted it, and I watched it slide out. As I fell, the 0.2 cam also pulled out, and I hit the ground on my left side.

Two climbers from Québec, certified EMTs, heard the fall and came over to assess and treat my injuries. I escaped with a laceration and abrasions to my left bicep, strained and torn groin muscles, and general bruising.

ANALYSIS

I should have been more cautious, given my relative inexperience on crack climbs. If I had asked one of the more experienced climbers to belay me, he might have been able to coach me about a bomber placement I missed about 30 feet up. My third placement could have been better, which would have prevented the ground fall; I was concerned about blocking holds, but if given the opportunity again, I would favor a more solid cam. I also should have truly tested the fourth cam before weighting it. (*Editor's note: Micro-cams generally have far less margin of error in their placements than larger cams. See "Essentials: Micro-cams" on page 39.*) Finally, when I started feeling uncomfortable I could have retreated, but I felt I had to push on. I should have lowered before I got pumped out. (*Source: Alan Jenn, 28.*)

MORE ADIRONDACKS INCIDENTS: *Data from several other incidents in the Adirondacks, including falls with injuries and two young climbers stranded at Poke-O-Moonshine when they attempted to rappel Catharsis with a single rope, are included in our tables.*

SHAWANGUNKS ANNUAL SUMMARY
Mohonk Preserve

In 2016 at the Mohonk Preserve there were 21 climbing-related incidents, including both injury and illness. Sixteen accidents required technical rescues. Seven of the accidents were caused by a belay system failure, while four were caused by inadequate protection. Three climbers suffered from heat-related illness.

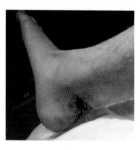

A climber sustained an unusual injury while on Star Action, a 5.10 in the Trapps. The climber fell while leading and collided with a non-locking carabiner attached to the last gear placement. The carabiner impaled the ankle and subsequently arrested the climber upside down from the heel. The climber removed the pierced carabiner and was lowered to the ground. (*Editor's note: A first-person report from this incident can be found at publications.americanalpineclub.org; search "Shawangunks snagged by carabiner." A similar accident occurred in West Virginia in 2016; see page 98.*)

Puncture wound from carabiner impalement.

Two climbers sustained multiple systems trauma while attempting to simul-rappel from Madam G's rappel stations. Uneven ropes caused one of these climbers to rappel off the rope, which led both climbers to drop approximately 20 feet to the ground. A stopper knot on both ends of the rappel line would have prevented the immediate cause of this accident. (*See page 44 for a detailed analysis of a similar incident in Yosemite Valley.*) Stopper knots or closing the system might have helped several other climbers avoid traumatic injuries from mistakes while rappelling or belaying in 2016.

A fatal accident occurred in the Near Trapps when a visitor was off-trail and fell over 100 feet to the ground. The cause of the fall is unknown. However, it is thought the visitor was by the cliff edge where soft duff provides poor traction—it's best to stay anchored or on belay until you've moved well back from the edge.

Several injuries were sustained while climbers were less than 10 feet off the ground, an environment where the perceived risk level was low. Confidence in our climbing abilities and in our partners can be the recipe for a great day. Confidence through complacency can also be our worst enemy. (*Source: Andrew Bajardi, chief ranger of Mohonk Preserve.*)

LONGER THAN EXPECTED TRAD FALL: *We did not receive a firsthand report, but there is a good account and analysis on Mountain Project of an incident on July 17 in which the leader took a long fall from the third-pitch crux of Shockley's Ceiling, despite protection quite close by, and suffered several fractures and a collapsed lung. The belayer, who weighed much less than the climber, "whipped violently up into the rock" while catching the fall and also sustained minor injuries. Other factors lengthening the fall may have included the leader adding extensions to the pieces he placed, slack in the belay, and rope stretch. (Belaying closer to the crux might be considered, in order to minimize stretch.) The incident is a reminder that many factors can add up to a much longer than expected fall.*

NORTH CAROLINA

LEADER FALL | Inadequate Protection
Linville Gorge Wilderness, Shortoff Mountain

During the morning of February 6, SO and his partner started the three-pitch classic Dopey Duck (5.9). Both were experienced climbers, and SO had climbed the route before. SO began leading the first pitch, placing three solid pieces. Somewhere above the third placement, he fell approximately 25 feet. He landed feet-first on the large pillar near the base of the climb before the rope came tight. He then swung back into the wall, striking his head and cracking his helmet. He suffered a tib/fib (lower leg) fracture.

SO's partner and other climbers on the scene provided care, stabilizing the patient and protecting against hypothermia. A HART (Helicopter Aquatic Rescue Team) crew out of Charlotte assisted in the rescue, helicoptering the patient from the base of the cliff. (*Source: Adrian Hurst.*)

ANALYSIS
Solid protection and a competent belayer are essential to reducing the risk of a fall. SO had both. However, it is also important to consider terrain features that may influence the outcome of a fall. Protection should be placed more frequently when close to the ground or above ledges. The helmet SO wore may have prevented another serious injury. (*Source: Aram Attarian.*)

ROCKFALL | Poor Position
Pisgah National Forest, Catheys Creek

During July, an organized group was climbing at Catheys Creek when it began to rain. The group leader moved the students under the shelter of an overhang. While waiting for the rain to stop, one of the teenage students reached up and grabbed a rock at head height to do a pull-up. The rock broke and came down on him and another student. Neither student lost consciousness or showed any signs of head trauma, but one stated he was unable to walk. Both students were carried out as a precaution, and the eventual diagnosis was pelvic fractures for one student and a bruised leg and hand trauma that required surgery for the other.

ANALYSIS

When working with groups, it's important for the leader or guide to familiarize himself or herself with the climbing site, including potential hazards associated with any staging area. Although this is one of those incidents that would have been almost impossible to predict, it might have been an opportunity to instruct students to test blocks, especially in overhangs, before one fully commits to any hold. (*Sources: Karsten Delap and Aram Attarian.*)

STRANDED | Inexperience, Darkness
Linville Gorge Wilderness, The Amphitheater

On September 17, four climbers set off to attempt the Prow (5.4), a classic three- or four-pitch route in the Amphitheater. All four had significant gym climbing experience. However, this would be their first time climbing outdoors on a multi-pitch

Approximate line of the Prow, showing the location of the stranded climbers at the end of the second pitch of the climb. *Mark Cushman*

trad route. The four divided into two teams, with the first starting up the route at approximately 8:30 a.m. They carried limited rock protection and insufficient clothing and water (all of their water was gone by 1 p.m.).

Both parties completed the first pitch without too much difficulty, although moving slowly. The second pitch presented some route-finding challenges for Pair 2, causing them to downclimb to the start of the pitch and start over. Both parties met at the top of the second pitch late in the day. By now it was getting dark, and the group had only two headlamps among the four climbers.

Pair 1 was able to complete the exposed finish of the climb with no difficulty, and they left a rope along the route to guide Pair 2 to the top. However, this rope was not secured and when Pair 2 pulled on it, the rope dropped and no longer showed the way. In darkness, Pair 2 attempted to continue but could not find the correct route. One of the climbers was cold and exhausted and refused to continue.

Pair 1 waited on top until well after dark before calling 911, in hopes that Pair 2 would be able to finish. Due to the distance and wind, Pair 1 lost voice contact with Pair 2, and they did not feel comfortable downclimbing to Pair 2's location. Pair 2 stayed on the large ledge at the top of pitch two and waited for rescue.

Rescuers arrived sometime after 11 p.m. Once voice contact and a visual on Pair 2's headlamp was established, a single rescuer rappelled directly to them. Pair 2 had an anchor with three well-placed cams and was secured behind boulders in an effort to get some relief from the wind. Clothing, water, and food were provided. Both individuals were uninjured but tired and frustrated with each other.

Rescuers atop the cliff set up a 3:1 haul system to assist the two climbers up the final pitch. The climbers were raised individually, taking approximately 30 minutes apiece. Assisted by rescuers, all the climbers then walked back to their vehicle. (*Source: James Robinson.*)

ANALYSIS

The 5.4 rating may have enticed these climbers to this route. Although the climb may be technically easy, the challenges of a tricky approach, route-finding, rope management, and traditional protection would make this a big step for climbers who are exclusively gym-trained. Finding an experienced mentor and/or building experience on shorter routes are more appropriate ways to venture onto new types of terrain. This incident is also a good reminder to carry adequate food, water, clothing, and headlamps for longer routes, even if you expect them to go quickly. (*Source: Aram Attarian.*)

GROUND FALL | Protection Pulled Out
Pilot Mountain, Veg-O-Matic

On September 17, a male climber, JC (23), took a ground fall that resulted in a medical evacuation. JC was leading Veg-O-Matic (5.7+ or 5.8), a one-pitch trad climb, when he fell approximately 40 feet to the ground. A climber on an adjacent climb observed the fall and called in the incident. He stated that JC was pulling the final overhang (and crux) of the route, just before reaching the fixed anchors, when he fell. A finger crack–size cam pulled out, failing to stop his fall.

Emergency medical services arrived at 2:40 p.m. The patient was able to answer questions about his name, day, time, birthday, and location but did not remember what had happened and continued throughout the rescue to ask how far he had fallen. Responders and park visitors began the carry-out at 3:24 p.m. JC was carried in a Stokes basket up the Ledge Springs Trail and then hauled with a pulley system up to the summit area. Here, he was placed into an ambulance. (*Source: Pilot Mountain State Park and Mountain Project.*)

ANALYSIS

Ample protection is available on this climb, suggesting the leader did not place enough pieces to prevent a ground fall when his cam pulled out. Small cams require experience for solid placements and should not be the sole piece preventing a major fall. It is not known if the patient was wearing a helmet. (*Source: Aram Attarian.*)

OREGON

FALL ON SNOW | Inadequate Protection, Failure to Self-Arrest
Mt. Hood, South Side Route

On June 9 a party of two experienced climbers (ages 49 and 52) fell high on the

Rescuers prepare to evacuate an injured climber after a fall while descending the Old Chute on the south side of Mt. Hood.
Endre Veka

South Side Route while descending the "Old Chute." The roped pair was unable to arrest the fall. One of the climbers suffered facial lacerations and bruised ribs. He was evacuated by a joint team from Portland Mountain Rescue and American Medical Response.

ANALYSIS
A roped team that does not belay or use intermediate running protection between climbers risks a group fall if any of the climbers slips. The decision of whether to rope up on steep snow depends on many factors, including the steepness and condition of the snow, the experience and skill of the climbers, the presence or absence of crevasses, and the presence of terrain traps below the climbers. Climbers must continuously assess the terrrain and conditions and adjust as necessary. (*Source: Jeff Scheetz, Portland Mountain Rescue, and the Editors.*)

LOST DURING DESCENT | Hypothermia, Frostbite
Mt. Hood, South Side Route

A party of four Seattle climbers left Timberline Lodge early Saturday morning, January 2, for a summit climb via the Wy'East Face. High winds, cold temperatures, and icy conditions slowed the ascent. The party summited at 3 p.m., and with superficial frostbite developing, they quickly descended the south side unroped, using headlamps. Two of the male members had previously climbed the route and led the descent. The party spread out, with the female member, age 27, lagging behind. The three male climbers reached the lodge, but the female member descended to the west of the lodge, heading toward the distant lights of Government Camp.

The lost climber called 911, which initiated a Portland Mountain Rescue (PMR) call-out. The climber texted a photo of a trail sign, which helped rescuers pinpoint her location. (A screenshot of the subject's phone showing a GPS location was inaccurate by about a half-mile and was disregarded.) She was located, assessed, and rewarmed by the PMR team and then assisted to Government Camp. Here, an American Medical Response team evaluated her for frostbite and hypothermia, and recommended transport to the hospital for treatment.

Allowing the party to separate during descent was a major mistake, especially given the development of frostbite and hypothermia in the female climber. Her off-route descent was likely due to unfamiliarity with the route and the difficulty of using navigation tools (compass and GPS receiver) due to the onset of hypothermia. Nonetheless, her phone was instrumental to the eventual rescue–a good reminder to keep some juice in the phone battery until you're off the mountain. (*Source: Jeff Scheetz, Portland Mountain Rescue.*)

FATAL FALL | Climbing Unroped
Mt. Washington

At around noon on June 30, Brian Robak (28) left Big Lake Youth Camp to attempt Mt. Washington (7,795 feet). Robak posted a social media photo confirming that he'd reached the summit at approximately 4:30 p.m. He was reported missing around 3 a.m. Searchers located personal possessions below Mt. Washington's standard route (the north ridge, 5.2) and his body was located via aircraft on July 2.

ANALYSIS
It is not possible to know the exact thought processes at play in this accident. The subject attempted the 5th-class descent from the summit without a rope or any protection. (This descent usually involves two rappels.) He was carrying a backpack and traveling in Converse Chuck Taylor shoes. There are no indications that he was off route. Weather was not a factor, and the fall most likely occurred during daylight hours. (*Source: Deschutes County Sheriff's Office Search and Rescue.*)

GROUND FALL
Smith Rock, Lower Gorge

A 37-year-old climber was leading Blood Clot (5.10b) on March 19 when he fell from approximately 15 feet up while attempting to clip his second piece of protection. The climber landed on the ground on his side and fractured his arm.

ANALYSIS
Pulling up rope to clip protection is a hazardous moment in a climb, especially close to the ground, since it adds significant slack to the belay system. If you're feeling insecure on a clipping stance, it's best to seek new holds (sometimes the next handhold up might be better for clipping), reposition your body for better balance, or downclimb to the previous piece or a stance for a rest. This climber was wearing a helmet, which possibly lessened the extent of his injuries. (*Source: Deschutes County Sheriff's Office Search and Rescue.*)

STRANDED IN MID-AIR | Off-Route Rappel
Smith Rock, Monkey Face

On June 22, Cordero Chavez (29) and Tyler Coleman (age unknown) climbed the Monkey Face spire via the Pioneer Route (5.7 C0). Upon completion of the climb, the

pair failed to identify the correct descent route. With their two ropes tied together, Coleman rappelled off the west side. (The standard rappel route is to the south.) Coleman reached the end of his ropes while free-hanging in space. (The rope ends were knotted.) Using the equipment on his harness, he was able to transfer his weight to a friction hitch around the rope, but even though he made several attempts to ascend the ropes, he was unable to make any real progress. Chavez dialed 911 from the summit when he was unable to communicate with his partner and the rope remained under tension for too long.

Rescuers responded and climbed the Pioneer Route to the summit. They hauled up 600-foot ropes to the top and performed a "pick-off" of the stranded climber on rappel, with a belay from above for backup. A rescuer and Coleman continued down the long ropes on the west face to reach the ground, while Chavez and the remaining rescuers descended the standard rappel route.

ANALYSIS
The guidebook and Internet are very clear on the proper descent route from the Monkey Face. These climbers actually climbed past both sets of descent anchors during their ascent. It's essential to carry and know how to use basic rope ascending gear when you venture onto climbs with increased commitment levels. (Source:: *Deschutes County Sheriff's Office Search and Rescue.*)

Rescuers ascend the Pioneer Route on Monkey Face to reach two stranded climbers. The rappel ropes of the climber who accidentally rappelled off the west face are highlighted in yellow. The stranded climber is out of sight below. *Matt Trager*

GROUND FALL | Inadequate Belay
Smith Rock, Morning Glory Wall

On November 12 at around 11 a.m., two experienced climbers were attempting Doritos (5.12c). One of the climbers (male, age 28) was leading the route when he fell off and the belayer (female, approximately 30) failed to arrest his fall. A witness observed the climber fall 50 to 60 feet and land on his belayer, who was knocked hard to the ground. Both the climber and the belayer sustained significant injuries, including head trauma, broken bones, spinal injury, abrasions, and burns.

ANALYSIS

There was a significant weight difference between the belayer and the heavier climber, which could have contributed to the belayer's inability to control the fall with her ATC-style device. However, belayers who weigh much less than their partners usually have little difficulty holding falls, and it seems likely there must have been a moment of inattention or distraction that caused the belayer to lose control. Another observer noted that the climber's fall was slow at first and then accelerated. The belayer was not wearing gloves, and the burn on her hand may have contributed to her being unable to regain control. An assisted-braking device might have helped her maintain the belay. The climber was wearing a helmet, but the belayer was not, possibly contributing to the severity of her injuries. (*Sources: Deschutes County Sheriff's Office Search and Rescue and Adam Lee.*)

RAPPEL ERROR | Uneven Ropes, No Stopper Knots
Smith Rock, Cocaine Gully

On November 21, a 31-year-old, moderately experienced climber had finished Deep Impact (5.10c), an 80-foot sport climb. She planned to rappel from the anchor. She established the rappel and started down, but 25 feet above the ground she rappelled off the end of one strand of the rope. The climber fell to the ground and sustained significant fractures to both lower legs and a shoulder injury.

ANALYSIS

For unknown reasons, the rope ends were uneven when the climber set up the rappel, and neither she nor her belayer noticed the problem. Before committing to a rappel, it's a good practice to ask people below, if possible, if both rope ends are down. No stopper knots were tied at the ends of each strand of rope. Although some climbers may feel that such knots are unnecessary for single-pitch rappels that end at the ground, in this case stopper knots likely would have prevented a serious accident. (*Sources: Deschutes County Sheriff's Office Search and Rescue and the Editors.*)

RAPPEL ERROR
Smith Rock, Rope de Dope Block

On November 24, after climbing Immortal Beloved (5.9), a climber fell about 35 feet to the ground upon unclipping from the anchor. The climber sustained lower leg fractures.

ANALYSIS

The exact error involved in this incident is unknown. Based on the scene after the fall, it appears that while cleaning the route the climber failed to thread his rope through the anchor correctly or inserted the rope strands into his rappel device incorrectly. When rappelling, always test that the system is set up properly by transferring your weight onto the rappel device and ropes *before* unclipping from the anchor. See "Essentials" on page 69. (*Source: Deschutes County Sheriff's Office Search and Rescue.*)

TENNESSEE

GROUND FALL | Inadequate Protection
Chattanooga, Suck Creek Canyon

Late in the morning on November 20, Josh Benti (26) and Jordan Tidbal-Sciullo (26) met Drew Bailey (39) at the Suck Creek climbing area and decided to climb a 5.8 offwidth (name unknown). While racking up, Josh noticed that no one in the group had any gear larger than a number 3 Black Diamond Camalot. Nevertheless, after a game of rock, paper, scissors to decide who would lead, Josh started up the climb, with Jordan belaying.

He placed his first piece at about seven feet. After climbing an additional 10 feet, he began to look for a second placement, but the crack was too wide for the number 3. After discussion with his partners on the ground, Josh decided to try to sling a chockstone in the crack at his waist. Drew tossed a sling up to Josh and he successfully girth-hitched the chockstone. However, while attempting to clip the rope, he lost his grip and fell approximately 20 feet to the ground, landing on his left shoulder and damaging his helmet. Josh was able to respond to questions and his breathing returned to normal, but during an assessment his partners noticed significant swelling in his right ankle. Josh was able to walk out with assistance from Jordan and Drew. Once at the hospital, it was revealed that Josh had broken his ankle.

ANALYSIS
Following the accident, the climbers noted there were a number of times when Josh could have backed down from the route. If you don't have the appropriate gear for a climb, pick a different route or just don't climb that day. When you're struggling to make a clip, it's sometimes best to back down to the previous piece or a stance, recover for a moment, and then return to the high piece to clip the rope. (*Sources: Josh Benti and the Editors.*)

TEXAS

FAILURE TO TIE IN
Austin, Reimers Ranch

On October 8, at the start of good climbing weather in Texas, I (36 years old) decided to start working on my 5.13 project for the season: Super Cruiser at Reimers Ranch, outside of Austin. At the end of the day we made our way to the climb. Three climbers were on the route next to us, and we casually talked about the day. One of them clipped the rope into the first and second bolts for me while he hung on his rope.

While I talked, I unconsciously tucked the free end of the rope into my harness. I never started tying in—I just didn't want the rope to swing away from me. I then went about my routine with my shoes and slowing my heart rate before beginning to climb. I never tied into the rope, but the rope moved with me as I set up. I took off my shirt to start, and my partner did not ask me to check my knot, nor did I check it myself—this is unusual for me.

I started up the route, which begins from a shelf about 10 feet off the ground and then moves up to a roof. I got to the second perma-draw, about 15 feet above the shelf, and then "took," hoping to rest. But the rope never came tight. Instead, I fell 15 feet and landed on the shelf, in a seated position, then bounced 10 feet to the ground, landing on my back. I had a compression fracture of my L5 vertebra and a chipped tooth. Somehow I did not hit my head (I did not have a helmet on). One of the climbers ran to the parking lot to call EMS and I was helicoptered to the hospital.

Super Cruiser (5.13a) at Reimers Ranch. The climber in this incident fell from the second bolt (P) and impacted the shelf visible in front of the belayer, then bounced 10 more feet to the ground. *John Hogge*

ANALYSIS

I was very lucky to have just a small fracture in my back and some bruises to show for my quick trip to the ground. I was walking in two days and back to work the next week.

I was distracted and talking too much. I was climbing with a trusted close friend. Our trust in each other doing the right thing led to complacency in our system. At any point, a quick knot check would have prevented the accident. Ultimately, the fault of this accident rests in my own distraction and not wanting to have to retrieve the rope if it swung out from the overhanging rock. Checking your knot and maintaining your system is important, no matter your experience. (*Source: Nathaniel Biggs.*)

UTAH

FATAL FALL ON SLAB | Climbing Unroped
Wasatch Range, Mt. Olympus

Celeste and her partner, both 36 and experienced climbers, were approaching the technical crux of Kamp's Ridge (5.6) on Mt. Olympus. It was a warm, sunny day around noon. They were in fourth-class terrain when Celeste fell approximately 100 feet. She impacted a low-angle slab and rolled a few times before striking her head on a rock. Her partner was able to call 911 and initiate a rescue, and then started to downclimb to reach her. A medical helicopter with a hoist was dispatched, but it had a mechanical issue and was unable to insert a nurse. A helicopter from the Utah Department of Public Safety was able to insert three members of the Salt Lake County SAR team, and they found Celeste deceased.

Celeste and her partner were amply experienced for this route. Her partner has done Kamp's Ridge many times and knew the route well. They were carrying a rope and rack for the crux pitches. However, the terrain they were in was low-angle and broken, which would make climbing with a rope difficult and create its own set of problems (snags, rockfall, etc.). I was a first responder at this accident, and I probably would have been climbing unroped in the area they were in.

A climber on Kamp's Ridge on Mt. Olympus. Broken, low-angled terrain like this is frequently scrambled unroped on long routes. *Jacob Moon*

Her partner didn't witness the start of the fall and is unsure if she pulled off a loose rock or slipped. She was not wearing a helmet when we arrived, but her partner had one and it's likely hers was removed before we got there. The blow she received was in the back and quite low, and many helmets wouldn't have offered much protection in this situation. This incident is a somber reminder of the risks we take while climbing. (Michael Finger, Salt Lake County Search and Rescue.)

HIGHBALL BOULDERING FALL
Big Cottonwood Canyon

A 30-year-old male had been bouldering with two other friends in an area near Lake Mary. The patient was attempting a hard and high new problem that he had previously top-roped a number of times. He fell from 20 to 30 feet, landed on his bouldering pads at an odd angle, and then rolled down a steep hillside for another 70 feet. The patient had wrist, head, back, and lower leg injuries.

ANALYSIS

All bouldering falls are ground falls. This climber was trying to get the first ascent of a hard highball (V–double digits?) that he had rehearsed on top-rope. The weather was cool and crisp, and the friction was good. This individual had many hard first ascents around Bishop, California, and beyond, and he knew the risks. A helmet for highballing might be worth considering? (*Source: Michael Finger, Salt Lake County SAR.*)

LOWERING ERROR | Rope Too Short, Failure to Close System
Little Cottonwood Canyon, The Egg

Salt Lake County Search and Rescue got called out at 2:36 p.m. on October 2 for a 35-year-old male climber who had fallen 30 or 40 feet after climbing Leggo My Eggo, a 5.10a bolted face on the Egg. He was believed to have broken or sprained his ankle. The fall occurred when the man's climbing partner was lowering him and let the end of the rope run through the belay device. The patient's fall stopped when he fell into some scrub oak, possibly saving him from worse injury. Rescuers lowered the patient to the foot of the wall, where he was packaged into a litter and carried to the parking lot.

ANALYSIS

Another climber was dropped while lowering from this same route a few years ago. This is a long pitch that requires a little downclimbing after lowering, even with a 70-meter rope. It's essential to close the belay system on the ground by tying a stopper knot in the belayer's end of the rope, tying the end to a rope bag, or having the belayer tie in. (*Sources: Michael Finger, Salt Lake County SAR, and the Editors.*)

FATAL TIE-IN ERROR IN MAPLE CANYON: *On July 23, an experienced climber died after falling to the ground from the anchor of a sport climb. We did not receive a firsthand report, but an online analysis from a close friend who was belaying at the time stated that the climber was likely distracted after passing the rope through the anchor chains. It is believed she threaded the rope through the tie-in points in her harness without beginning or completing her usual retraced figure-8 knot. She is believed to have tied an overhand knot, intended as a backup, that briefly held her weight after she unclipped her tethers and before she fell.*

LEADER FALL ON ICE | Ice Tool Puncture Wound
Little Cottonwood Canyon, Snowbird

I was on Rookie Party in Pipeline Bowl, above the Snowbird ski resort, on October 23. This is a WI4 single-pitch ice climb at about 10,500 feet. Ice conditions weren't great, but other than messing with my head, the conditions did not play a role in my fall. The total climb is around 220 feet, but it is mostly low-angle except for a 35- to 40-foot vertical section in the lower portion. I had placed several screws and rock pro prior to and through the vertical section. My last placement was a 13 cm screw in solid ice, about six feet from the top of the vertical section. Climbing on half ropes, I clipped one of the ropes through a quickdraw attached to that screw.

At the top of the vertical section, with my tools over the lip, I was moving my feet up to make the final moves when my right tool popped out. My weight was back, so this sent me backward. My left tool was still engaged in the ice. I assume I let go of it, but I can't really remember. I yelled "Falling!" and soon found myself upside down, with my head about five feet above a lower-angle section of the climb. The top screw had held, but combining my height above the screw, the stretch in the skinny rope, slack in the rope, and the distance my belayer went up the mountain, it added up to about a 30-foot fall.

I righted myself and lowered off the route. After a few sighs of relief and a hug to my belayer, I untied from the ropes and took a few steps. Blood started to pour down the inside of my leg. In a few seconds there were two 12-inch pools of blood in the snow. The wound was a puncture high on the back of my leg—basically my butt, close to my crotch. We put pressure on it for about 20 minutes, but it was still bleeding. Two of our team went for help, and another (who was a nurse) stayed with me.

Courtesy of Black Diamond

The Snowbird resort sent two patrollers, and four Salt Lake County Search and Rescue members responded as well. After an hour and a half of direct pressure the bleeding had stopped. Not wanting to risk walking for fear of starting the bleeding again, one of the rescuers belayed me while I slid down 200 feet of steep snow toward a boulder field. About six hours after the fall, I was picked up by a helicopter and flown off the mountain.

ANALYSIS

I believe that I let go of my left tool as I started to fall and this tool remained in the ice until it was overloaded through my umbilical. (*Ice climbers sometimes attach stretchy "umbilicals" to leashless tools to tether them to their harness, so the tool is retrievable if dropped.*) I believe either my crampon placement or one of the ropes caused me to flip upside down. Somewhere during that transition, the loaded ice tool snapped out of the ice and the pick impacted my leg. The tool either hit me directly as it released from the ice or shot past me and then rebounded into my leg. The puncture was one inch wide by 1.5 inches deep. It was definitely not from a screw and could not have been a crampon point, since it was too high on my butt.

Other than during a couple of long alpine routes, I had never climbed with umbilicals until this. But I also had never fallen on ice before this. After this injury, I will no longer be using umbilicals on single-pitch routes. I feel like I was actually pretty lucky. The fall alone could have been much worse, and the tool could have easily impacted my head, neck, or abdomen. (*Source: Brett Verhoef.*)

EDITOR'S NOTE: *As with many decisions in climbing, the choice of when to use umbilicals on ice tools (or leashes, for that matter) varies with the situation and the climber. Keep in mind that a dropped tool could have serious consequences for the leader even on a single-pitch climb, if he or she is unable to find protection or an anchor. Belayers and bystanders below also might be at risk.*

As other reports in this edition will attest, there are potentially far more serious consequences than a puncture wound for the leader who falls off an ice climb. Outside of modern, bolt-protected dry-tooling routes, the generations-old safety rule for ice climbing is still valid: The leader must not fall. Expert climber and author Will Gadd wrote an excellent blog post about avoiding ice climbing falls in January 2017; search for "Note to self: How not to fall off ice climbing."

ANCHOR FAILURE | Poor Rock, No Backup
Canyonlands National Park, Maze District

On May 25, Brent Blakenburg (30), Jason Bernard (36), Sean Finnegan (27), and Daniel Coldfelter (36) were camped near the Hans Flat Ranger Station in the Maze District of Canyonlands National Park. The Maze is well known for its remote location (about 40 miles from the nearest paved road). In the morning, Bernard began checking out a bouldering route at the base of a 50-foot sandstone outcropping. A summary based on Bernard's notes follows.

We had been looking at possible routes up several faces on the rock, and eventually Dan and I decided to see if we could anchor a top-rope and attempt a possible first ascent on this bulging mound. Right above the most viable route was an amazing horn. I wrapped 10 feet of webbing, tied with a water knot, around a three-foot hunk of the rock; there was a perfect crease to lock the webbing into position. I attached a quick-link and prepared the rope. As I dropped the top-rope to the ground, Dan and I spoke briefly about setting up a backup anchor but decided there were not any reliable gear placements. And the horn appeared bomber.

I weighted the rope to test it while standing on the ground, then Dan tied in and began climbing. He had some trouble with the beginning moves, resulting in a few swinging falls, and asked me to tie in. I also took a swinging fall on the sandy, traversing route. I weighted the rope again on a fall as I moved toward the anchor, cleaning off about eight grapefruit-size holds as I went. After completing the route, I was lowered off the climb.

Brent now tied in. When he was about 30 feet above the ground, a handhold broke and Brent fell off. Sean, who was belaying, caught the fall. However, the horn that had been slung as an anchor, plus a three-foot-wide section of the surrounding rock, sheared off the wall. Brent fell to the ground, narrowly missing being crushed by the blocks falling around him.

Brent remained conscious and moved under his own power away from the base of the climb. An initial scan found blood on his head, a bloody nose, and a thigh laceration. He pointed out that his left ankle was disfigured, so Sean removed the climbing shoe from that foot. As the shoe was removed, the pad of Brent's heel fell into my hand, exposing muscle and bone. We used clothing and a towel to bind up Brent's ankle and heel, and quickly prepared to

REMOTE 911 CALLS

Even if your cell phone is showing no bars, it's always worth attempting a 911 emergency call in remote areas.

- All carriers are required to provide free 911 service, and another carrier might be able to connect your call even if your carrier has no service in the area.
- An attempted 911 call may leave digital breadcrumbs of time, date, and location information that searchers can access and use, even if your call never connects.
- If you're connected, immediately tell the emergency operator your location and phone number, in case you are disconnected. If you're disconnected and no one calls back, try again.

evacuate. During the 40-mile drive out of the backcountry, I was able to connect with emergency services via my cell phone. An ambulance met us en route and determined that an airlift to the hospital in Grand Junction was warranted, given the extent of Brent's injuries. He reached the hospital only two hours after the accident and recovered well.

ANALYSIS

"Looking at the scene of the accident later that day, it was easy to see there were mistakes made in choosing the horn as a top-rope anchor, and we probably should not have even tried climbing [in this area] at all due to the loose rock." A backup might have prevented Blakenburg's ground fall, but he also might have been hit by a large piece of rock if he hadn't fallen out of its way; a boulder impacted right where he'd been climbing. The bottom line: Some rock just isn't meant to be climbed.

These climbers correctly completed an assessment of Blakenburg's injuries prior to evacuation. A full patient assessment is important to avoid overlooking injuries. Disfigured limbs or bloody wounds often distract from other potentially serious issues, such as neck and spinal injuries, especially in ground falls. (*Sources: Jason Bernard and the Editors.*)

LEADER FALL | Loose Rock, Chopped Rope
Indian Creek Canyon, Bridger Jack, Hummingbird Spire

On November 14, Kelsey Brasseur (29) and I (28) planned to climb all of Indian Creek's Bridger Jack towers in a day. By 3 p.m. we had dispatched four of the towers and arrived at the base of Hummingbird Spire, where we ran into an acquaintance, Andrew, and his partner. After swapping pleasantries, Kelsey and I started up Hoop Dancer (5.11). Kelsey led the first pitch and I met her at the large belay ledge. Without glancing at the topo or even looking up, I grabbed the rack and took off toward the summit.

I deemed the rock too loose for any useful protection, so I ran it out up moderate terrain for 15 to 20 feet above the belay. (I later found out I was off route.) Knocking on each loose block before I grabbed it—all of them rang with a hollow sound—I picked the best hold I could find and pulled down. A cooler-size rock dislodged and fell toward the ledge below, with me underneath. The block hit the ledge and exploded on top of me as I bounced off and continued downward, ripping out the anchor piece through which I'd been redirected.

Twenty feet below the ledge, I jerked to a stop, hanging upside down by the rope around my ankle. I glanced down and saw a six-foot tail of rope coming from my harness. The rope had been cut in the fall. One of the smaller chunks of rock that had rained down with the block had fallen directly into a wide crack on the belay ledge and wedged itself in as a chockstone, somehow catching a section of rope. My foot was caught inside this 10-foot loop, holding me only around the top of my instep. My right arm was clearly broken, as my radius had come through my skin.

Kelsey removed the Grigri from the lead side of the rope, unburied the rope from the debris on the ledge, and fixed the longest line of undamaged rope to the anchor. She then rappelled about 10 to 15 feet toward me. I asked her to secure the rope holding me, which was somewhat precariously seated around the chockstone and led to my ankle, and to throw down a line for me to secure myself.

She wrapped the loose section of the snagged rope, above the chockstone, around her right hand, taking as much weight as possible in case the chockstone dislodged. She used her left hand to gather up another length of undamaged rope and lower it with a locking carabiner on a bight. I snatched the rope and pulled it down toward my harness, but it was slightly too short.

I pulled myself up with my good arm, grabbed the carabiner with my broken arm, and flopped my lifeless arm toward my harness. After several unsuccessful attempts to land the carabiner on my belay loop, I landed it on my left leg loop. Worried I wouldn't be able to get to my belay loop before my good arm completely gave out, I clipped the leg loop.

Kelsey was still holding the rope around my ankle. In order for her to reach the anchor and fix the rope I was now clipped in to, I needed to get my

Hummingbird Spire. The accident occurred in the notch at right. *Brad Brandewie*

weight off the rope. After talking with Kelsey, I reached over to the flared chimney on my right, rammed my broken pelvis in as far as I could, and chicken-winged my broken arm to establish myself. Kelsey released the rope around her hand and quickly fixed the rope that was attached to my leg loop. As soon as I weighted the leg loop and swung out, I enchained some cams from the bight in the fixed rope to my belay loop (although I was still hanging off my leg loop).

Having heard the rockfall, Andrew ran around the corner to the base of Hummingbird. I told him our rope was too damaged to get us down on our own. He raced down the talus to his car and sped toward the Canyonlands National Park ranger station.

As I hung by my leg loop, Kelsey gathered more rope to lower herself further down and pull me over to a small ledge on my right, where we rigged up a series of slings to stabilize my legs.

An hour or two later, Andrew returned and let us know that rescue was on the way. It was now dark, but Andrew racked up, climbed the first pitch, and built an anchor above us, planning to lower me to the ground. We had a hard time getting me off the ledge, both because of pain and because we were trying to hold my body still, out of fear of spinal cord injury. After a discussion, I decided it was worth the risk to lower down without a backboard, reasoning that A) it could be a very long time before SAR would be able to rig up a safe lowering setup (if they were able to do this at all); B) further movement would pale in comparison to any movement/ trauma I'd already undergone; and C) although I was not bleeding too much, we were aware of the risk of hypovolemic shock.

Andrew did a great job of lowering me slowly and communicating, allowing me time to stabilize as I descended. About three hours after the fall, I was back on the ground. Perhaps half an hour after that, a paramedic showed up, then two flight nurses in another half an hour. The flight nurses injected me with a steady dose of ketamine for the long carry down the talus.

I sustained a broken pelvis (inferior ramus, superior ramus, and acetabulum), broken back (burst L1), a broken sacrum, broken arm (open radial fracture), dislocated wrist, and damage to my sacral nerves. (*Source: Craig Gorder.*)

ANALYSIS

Because the two climbers were moving fast to accomplish their linkup, Gorder neglected to check the route topo to see where the line went, and as a result he got off route on rotten rock, but he continued without protection because the terrain was easy for him.

Gorder was wearing a helmet, which he credits with saving his life, as the helmet had a sizable depression in it and he came away with no head trauma. He had also just taken a wilderness first responder (WFR) course, which allowed him to assess his own injuries, remain calm, and take the lead in decision-making. (Since he was fully conscious and aware, he explained, he didn't want his partner to be forced to make serious decisions affecting him.) Gorder also said that bringing a SPOT or similar communication device to this isolated cliff could have sped up the arrival of paramedics.

All of these climbers can be commended for their handling of a shocking and extraordinary accident. (*Source: The Editors.*)

INDIAN CREEK RAPPEL ERROR: *A report about a fatal rappelling accident in March can be found at publications.americanalpineclub.org. Search "Mark Davis rappel."*

RAPPEL ERROR | Climbing Alone
Zion National Park, Moonlight Buttress

On the afternoon of March 9, two climbers on the Moonlight Buttress route reported that someone had fallen from above them. Rangers investigated and located the body of a male at the base of the climb. This individual, Eric Klimt, 36, was wearing a harness and climbing shoes, and he had a closed Grigri belay device clipped to the belay loop of his harness.

It is possible to hike to the top of Moonlight Buttress via the West Rim Trail. Investigators found that the climber had fixed a 70-meter rope to the top anchor on the climb, rappelled to the next anchor down, and fixed the rope again there. It is common practice to fix the upper pitches of Moonlight Buttress in order to practice free climbing with a self-belay system. It appears this is what the subject was planning to do. Other than the rope and the gear he was carrying when he fell, the rest of the climber's gear remained on the rim.

While the exact cause of the fall will never be known, the evidence suggests he either rappelled off the end of the rope or made an error while transferring from the rappel rope to an anchor or vice-versa. There was no knot tied in the end of the rope. There also did not appear to be any kind of backup on the rope or harness.

A knot at the end of the rope on rappels, especially where it is known that the rope does not reach the ground, adds a safety backup that may prevent a person from rappelling off the end of the rope. A friction hitch such as an autoblock or prusik, tied around the rope and clipped to the harness, provides another form of backup. When transferring from an anchor to a fixed line or rappel rope, and vice versa, it's essential to weight and test the new connection before unclipping from the previous system. Although it's not certain if any of these steps would have prevented this tragedy, they are known to prevent many rappelling and self-belay accidents. (*Source: Ranger Andrew P. Fitzgerald, Zion National Park.*)

WASHINGTON

LOWERING ERRORS | Rope Too Short
Index, Lower Town Wall

In April, I was climbing at Index with my girlfriend and her family. I had run up the route Godzilla (5.9) to put up a top-rope for them. At the last second her parents asked us to hang their rope instead of ours. I didn't think about it, but their rope was 60 meters and mine was a 70. I was climbing in approach shoes and everyone was chatting at the base—super casual, very relaxed. As I was lowering, we ran out of rope a few meters above the ground and my belayer accidentally let the end of the rope run through her brake hand. I dropped a few meters onto pretty gnarly rocks, landing on my butt and side and injuring my back a bit (compression fracture of two vertebrae).

ANALYSIS
Lots of things should have been done better: We should have thought about how long the rope was, we should have been paying more attention, and we should have had a knot in the end of the rope. I wasn't wearing a helmet and was lucky to not injure my head—had I landed on my head, it probably would have been disastrous. My belayer had been climbing less than a year. Basically, things were all just a bit too lax. (*Source: Alex Honnold.*)

BIKE CRASH DURING DESCENT FROM CLIMB
North Cascades, North Twin Sister Mountain

I climbed the classic west ridge of North Twin Sister Mountain near Mt. Baker on a fine August day. It was very warm and I got a late start. As many do, I used a mountain bike for the approach, which follows about nine kilometers of logging roads. The final part of this is an overgrown road that becomes a climbers' trail. I left my bike at the trail.

I summited at 6:30 p.m. and downclimbed the fourth-class ridge safely while it was light, but it was dark when I got to my mountain bike. At this point, I was out of food and almost out of water, and was looking forward to the mostly downhill ride to the car. Although it occurred to me that my headlamp was poor illumination for downhill mountain biking, I got on the bike anyway. Within 200 meters I had an over-the-handlebars wipeout, breaking two ribs on my left side. After collecting myself and realizing I was not severely injured, and that my bike still worked, I cautiously and painfully rode out to my car.

ANALYSIS

As I was climbing alone (but within my ability and tolerance level for exposure), I took considerable care on the ascent and descent, but I let my guard down a bit once I started to hike out. This accident occurred on the descent, after all the major difficulties were behind me, which seems very typical of many mountain accidents and is why I am submitting this report. Also, many climbers occasionally use bikes for accessing the alpine. Riding in the dark when one is tired and on unfamiliar ground has risks that should not be underestimated, especially when alone. (*Source: DG, male, age 56.*)

RAPPEL FAILURE | Inadequate Knot
Methow Valley, Goat Wall, Prime Rib of Goat

About 3:30 p.m. on May 3, Ryan Kautz, 26, was rigging a rappel off Prime Rib of Goat, a multi-pitch 5.9 bolted route, with new 70-meter, 9.5mm ropes. He and his two partners had seen a storm coming in and decided to descend after climbing eight of the 11 pitches. One of the partners had managed the ropes on the previous rappels, and Kautz asked to take over at the second-to-last anchor. The two other climbers waited on a ledge 50 feet away (it's necessary to scramble down to the anchor from the previous stance).

Kautz slipped one end of the rope through a chain anchor and tied it to an identical rope. He tested the rappel by tugging on it and then lowered himself about 20 feet before something went wrong. His partners heard a loud snap and saw Kautz fall 100 feet and disappear into a gully. The other climbers were able to get help from a climbing guide above, who fixed a rope so one of Kautz' partners could rappel into the gully. Kautz was found dead roughly 90 minutes after his fall. He was still attached to the ropes, his rappel device was properly threaded, and there was no damage to either rope. (*Source: Rock and Ice magazine.*)

ANALYSIS

During the previous rappels the climbers had used a flat figure-8 knot to join their two ropes, backed up with overhand knots on either side of the flat figure-8. Although Kautz' partners did not see him tie the final knot, it's likely he too used a flat figure-8; it's unknown if he backed up the knot. Testing has shown the flat figure-8 is prone to rolling or "capsizing" under loads and is therefore not recommended for rappelling. (The new ropes in this incident reportedly had a very slick dry coating, possibly making it easier for the flat figure-8 to fail.) A properly tied and dressed flat overhand with long tails, a double fisherman's, or a Flemish bend (retraced figure-8) are reliable ways to join rappel ropes.

The distance between the climbers before the fateful rappel also contributed to this accident. This reportedly was Kautz' first multi-pitch climb, and he would have benefitted from a more experienced partner checking his rappel setup. (*Source: The Editors.*)

STRANDINGS | Weather, Altitude Sickness
Mt. Rainier, Disappointment Cleaver and Emmons Glacier

In the first three weeks of the summer season on Rainier, rangers performed three helicopter rescues. The first was on June 10, after two climbers spent several unplanned nights on the summit after becoming disoriented.

The second rescue was June 19, two days after a pair of climbers summited via the Disappointment Cleaver route but were caught in a storm as they descended. They dug a snow cave just below the crater rim, at 14,300 feet, and activated a SPOT locator beacon twice on June 17. Search crews were unable to reach them until June 19, due to severe conditions, so they spent two nights in single-digit temperatures. Both climbers were in stable condition when rescued.

Just before midnight on June 27, a team left Camp Schurman at 9,450 feet to attempt the summit via the Emmons Glacier route. A 23-year-old climber reported feeling ill before they reached the top, so they descended to 11,500 feet. The climb-

er was having trouble breathing and couldn't continue descending, so one person remained with the ill climber while the rest of the team went down to Camp Schurman to call for help on a park service emergency radio. That same day, a helicopter dropped rangers onto a ledge several hundred feet below the stranded climbers and they climbed up to the pair. The climbers were extracted by short haul to a landing zone, flown to the base of the mountain, and the patient was transferred to an ambulance for a trip to the hospital to be checked out. (*Source: Mt. Rainier National Park.*)

Short-haul training: A climbing ranger brings in the rope during a training exercise near the Tahoma Glacier on Mt. Rainier. *Julian Hanna / NPS Photo*

ANALYSIS

Such incidents demonstrate how important it is to carry the necessary equipment and clothing to survive several unplanned nights high on the mountain, including a tent or shovel for building an emergency snow cave and a stove to melt snow for water. A personal locator beacon is the surest way to call for help; a system that allows two-way communication can greatly facilitate rescue efforts. Finally, in the case of altitude illness, descent is the best treatment; an early decision to turn around when a climber shows signs of acute mountain sickness can avoid more serious illness and/or the need for rescue. (*Source: The Editors.*)

EXPOSURE, HYPOTHERMIA
Mt. Rainier, Gibraltar Ledges

About 10 p.m. on March 26, people at Camp Muir notified rangers that two climbers had not returned from their summit bid and their gear was still in the shelter. At 9:30 a.m., Monique Richard, 41, could be heard yelling for help above Camp Muir.

After she was helped down to camp, she said that she and her partner, Arvid Lahti, 58, had been caught in a storm while descending. They sought shelter below a ridge near Gibraltar Ledges, but Lahti succumbed overnight from hypothermia. The storm had included wind gusts estimated to 83 mph and temperatures near 0°F. Richard also suffered from hypothermia but survived. Rescuers found Lahti's body at about 10,600 feet, 400 vertical feet above Camp Muir.

ANALYSIS

Lahti and Richard were both experienced climbers who had completed multiple high-altitude peaks. (Lahti was a well-known Norwegian mountaineer.) As visitors to the area, they may have been on a tight time schedule. However, they should have paid closer attention to the weather forecast, which called for a significant winter storm to start during the afternoon of their climb. They may not have seen this forecast, or perhaps the reasonably good weather at Camp Muir on the morning of their ascent prompted them to attempt a rapid climb and descent, before the storm arrived. It's also possible their background led them to underestimate a winter climb of Rainier, which requires good conditions, stable weather, and the clothing and equipment to survive an unexpected storm or delay. (*Sources: Mt. Rainier National Park, media accounts, and the Editors.*)

OTHER WASHINGTON INCIDENTS: *Complete reports were not received for several other serious accidents in Washington state in 2016, including a solo climber who died after a long fall on Mt. Adams and a woman who fell while climbing in Icicle Creek Canyon. These incidents and others are included in our data tables for the year.*

WEST VIRGINIA

RAPPEL ERRORS | Inexperience, Inadequate Backup
Seneca Rocks, East Face, Bee Sting Corner

On April 17 an inexperienced male climber (age unknown), a member of a three-person team, was rappelling for his first time from the anchor atop Bee Sting Corner (5.7). A more experienced climber rappelled first and was at the base when the accident occurred. The climber reportedly rigged the rappel device correctly, had an autoblock backup, and was wearing fingerless gloves. During the descent, the climber lost control of his brake hand and slid approximately 100 feet to the right side of a ledge at the start of the Skyline Traverse, sustaining a fractured ankle. The autoblock did not engage during this rapid descent. No fireman's belay was applied by his partner at the base of the rappel. (*Sources: Mountain Project and Arthur Kearns.*)

ANALYSIS

Based upon secondhand reports, the person likely lost control while negotiating a small roof approximately 15 feet down the rappel, perhaps in an attempt to avoid hitting the lip of the roof. The climber applied only two wraps of an autoblock as a backup. The inadequate backup and failure of the partner on the ground to observe and apply a fireman's belay to the rappel strands were contributing factors.

Between 2000 and 2011, 11.3 percent of all rappel incidents reported in *Accidents* were attributed to poor technique, while another 19.4 percent were due to inadequate backups. (See "Know the Ropes," *Accidents* 2012). In this case, either the two wraps of the autoblock were not enough to "grab" the rope or the autoblock may have been placed in close proximity to the rappel device, preventing it from arresting the rappeller after the loss of control. The rappeller could have employed other techniques to assist in maintaining control, including applying more friction in the system (e.g., wrapping the rope around his body). (*Source: The Editors.*)

THUMB AMPUTATED BY ROPE IN FALL
New River Gorge, Cotton Top

Just after 5 p.m. on May 12, a male climber (age 29) was attempting to lead Cottonmouth, a 5.10a sport climb at Cotton Top, a small crag on the north side of the New River Gorge. The climber moved quickly through the lower portion of the climb. Once he was within arm's reach of the fifth bolt, he clipped a quickdraw to the bolt hanger. Taking slack in the rope, the climber attempted to clip the draw with his right hand and at that point fell approximately 20 feet. At some point during the fall, the rope encircled the climber's left thumb, and when the rope came taut the thumb was amputated at the midpoint of the proximal phalange (just above the MCP joint, the second of the three joints in the thumb).

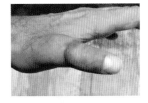

Good decisions after this accident allowed surgical reattachment of the thumb.

The climber was immediately lowered by his belayer (24). The climber and belayer retrieved the thumb—first identified on the ground by the climber's dog—and placed it in a water bottle filled with cold water. The climber removed his shirt, applied pressure to the thumb, and raised his hand above his heart. After stopping to place the amputated portion of the thumb in a plastic bag, surrounded by ice, the climbers immediately went to a local hospital and eventually to a specialized hand-surgery center in Louisville, Kentucky, where the thumb was successfully reattached during a four-hour surgery beginning at 1 a.m. on May 13. (*Source: R. Bryan Simon, from interview with the injured climber.*)

ANALYSIS
Sometimes in climbing, as in life, bad things happen. In this case the climber took a fall similar to many others experienced daily across the United States. The climber could not recall grabbing for the rope with his left hand, though this may be the case. (Grabbing the rope should always be avoided while falling.) Once the accident occurred, the climbers made a series of good decisions that resulted in saving the victim's thumb. From placing pressure on the wound to placing the amputated thumb in clean, cool water, to wrapping it in plastic and storing it with ice, to rapidly evacuating to medical care, and finally to self-identifying a hospital with well-trained hand specialists, calm decision-making allowed a successful reattachment, preserved function of the thumb, and allowed the patient to return to climbing and other outdoor activities just three months after the incident. (*Source: R. Bryan Simon.*)

INDOOR CLIMBING FINGER AMPUTATION: *In September, an experienced climber in Colorado had the index finger of his right finger amputated in similar fashion during a leader fall in a gym. The climber wrote in a post at Mountain Project: "I am not one to grab my rope during a lead fall, and I take hundreds of lead falls per year. My belayer knows what she is doing; she has also been climbing for many years. The way I see it, it is a 'freak accident,' one that could not have been prevented." Surgeons reattached this climber's finger, but complications forced a surgical amputation three days later.*

LEADER FALL | 'Sticky' Cam Pulled Out
New River Gorge, Bridge Buttress

On the afternoon of May 22, a female climber (age unknown) was attempting to lead the route Layback, a 5.9+ trad climb at the popular Bridge Buttress area. The climber took a short fall, loading her highest piece, a finger-size cam, which then pulled from the placement. The climber's fall continued approximately 12 feet onto a ledge, with the initial impact being absorbed by her right foot, before the climber inverted and her fall was arrested just prior to hitting the ground.

The initial impact resulted in an open fracture that displaced the right foot laterally, exposed and damaged portions of her lower tibia and fibula, severed surrounding connective tissue, and introduced a large amount of environmental debris to the wound. After lowering the climber to the ground, the belayer conducted initial care for the injured limb, assessing for circulation, sensation, and movement (which were all intact). Additionally, he supported the injured limb, shielded it from the climber in an effort to calm her, and called for assistance. Responders transported the patient to an ambulance. (*Source: Jeff Hearn, New River Alliance of Climbers.*)

ANALYSIS
Post-accident inspection of the spring-loaded camming device (SLCD) that pulled out showed no significant physical damage, deformation, or misalignment of any parts. However, the movement of the cam lobes on the axle was slow and unresponsive. During a fall, a cam's springs and the friction between the lobes and the rock are what hold the cam in place before the downward force on the cam stem translates into outward force on the lobes. "Sticky" cams with reduced motion in the lobes thus are easier to pull out of a crack, especially in slippery or polished rock. To ensure optimal performance, SLCDs should be regularly inspected, cleaned, and lubricated (using a wax- or graphite-based lubricant), and the trigger wires should be straightened so the lobes open and contract easily and smoothly. (*Source: The Editors.*)

UNTIMELY FALL SNAGS FOOT WITH CARABINER
New River Gorge, Meadow River

On June 29, Chad Watkins (age 49) was attempting Big Top, a 5.12a trad climb in the Greatest Show area of the Meadow River Gorge. The nature of the crack requires foot placements near and just above gear. As Chad attempted the crux, his left foot popped from the crack and came into contact with the lower carabiner of the quickdraw attached to his uppermost nut placement. The nose of the carabiner penetrated the back of his foot, just forward of the Achilles tendon, and caught on the Achilles and calcaneus (heel), thus arresting his fall. (His belayer, Amanda Smith, said she felt no weight come onto the rope.) Chad managed to pull himself up off the carabiner and was lowered to the ground.

Nearby climbers, including a paramedic, assessed his injury, dressed the wound, and assisted in evacuation to the parking area using a two-man rope litter. Amazingly, Chad suffered no permanent damage—he received three stitches in the ER and was walking the next day and climbing within the week. (*Sources: Chad Watkins, Amanda Smith, Jeremy Fox, and Chad Heddleston.*)

ANALYSIS
The nature of the holds on this route required Chad to position his foot near his previous gear placements, and very likely running behind his rope. In this instance, there were no real options other than to continue to move up the route. (*Editor's note: A very similar accident occurred in the Shawangunks in 2016; the report is available at publications.americanalpineclub.org.*) While an impalement hazard like this would be very difficult to foresee, it could be avoided by clipping the piece to the rope with a locking carabiner.

Although it was not the case in this incident, there have been reports of penetrating injuries from climbers deliberately grabbing gear, usually quickdraws, to prevent a fall. This practice should be avoided as it may result in puncture wounds or degloving injuries (the traumatic removal of large areas of skin on the fingers or hand). Seeking better stances or holds, attempting to downclimb, or falling with hands outstretched usually is preferred over grabbing gear. (*Source: The Editors.*)

LEADER FALL, LOST TOOTH
Summersville Lake, Long Wall

At 4 p.m. on April 8, Connor Damato (age 21) was attempting to lead Jesus Is My License Plate (5.10d), a sport route on Long Wall. This was Damato's first outdoor roped climbing experience and his first day of lead climbing. He and his partner had been climbing all day.

Damato's partner attempted to lead the pitch but stopped at the second bolt and was lowered. Damato then began the route, moving through the lower sections of the climb without difficulty. He was above the fifth bolt, attempting to clip the anchors, when he fell.

WHAT TO DO ABOUT KNOCKED-OUT TEETH

- Do not scrub, disinfect, or allow the root of a dislodged tooth to dry out.
- Rinse the tooth with saline or water to remove debris; do not touch the root.
- Re-implant the tooth right away, if possible. Push the tooth into the socket; hold it in place with your fingers or by gently biting down.
- If unable to reposition the tooth, store it in milk or your saliva (possibly in cheek). See a dentist as soon as possible (ideally within 30 minutes). The longer the tooth is out, the less chance for successful re-implantation.

Source: Auerbach's Wilderness Medicine, 7th Edition

Damato was positioned an arm's length below and to the left of the anchor and had just placed a quickdraw through the leftmost anchor bolt. He had pulled up slack in the rope and held it with his teeth before clipping the rope in the draw. At this point he fell. Due to the slack in the system and his belayer standing away from the base of the wall, he fell approximately 35 feet. His fall was arrested approximately four feet from the ground. During the fall, Damato instinctively bit down on the rope, and as the rope jerked free it pulled one tooth completely from his mouth and fractured and impacted another tooth into his gum line. The climbers were unable to locate the missing tooth.

ANALYSIS

This was the first outdoor climbing trip for Connor, who said he mainly bouldered in the gym. He and his partner should have scaled back their expectations rather than attempt a climb that was beyond their abilities. Though Damato suffered no other injuries, the fall distance could have been lowered by the belayer standing closer to the wall during the lead belay. It's important to have a solid clipping stance when holding slack with your teeth, or else try to move to a stance that avoids this method altogether. (*Sources: Connor Damato, R. Bryan Simon.*) *Editor's note: A similar incident occurred at Indian Creek, Utah, in 2016. The climber, a dental hygienist, had two teeth dislodged and one knocked out but saved all three teeth with quick action.*

DEEP WATER SOLOING INJURY
Summersville Lake, Rats Hole

The PsicoRoc 2016 competition at Summersville Lake. *Gabe DeWitt*

At 7 p.m. on August 23, Jesse Grupper (age 18) was attempting an unclimbed project (now 5.13d) during the first deep water solo competition on real rock in the United States: PsicoRoc 2016 at Summersville Lake. After successfully negotiating the climb to the final move, Grupper fell approximately 55 feet and landed feet-first in the water below.

Multiple witnesses reported that Grupper seemed to bend forward just before impact, causing his upper body and head to impact the water at a slight angle. Upon surfacing, he was picked up by an event watercraft, whose driver immediately called for the medical team to evaluate Grupper. He was transferred to the medical support boat, evaluated for injuries, and evacuated to a nearby hospital. Grupper was determined to have suffered a concussion and a broken tooth from the impact of the fall. (*Source: Seth Hawkins, MD, and Deb Simon, RN, Vertical Medicine Resources.*)

ANALYSIS

This fall was from a height greater than previous ones during the competition, and the additional height was most likely the primary cause of the injury. Grupper may have expected an earlier landing and looked down in anticipation, causing his upper torso to angle forward and impact the water upon entry. During the rescue, the climber's spinal motion was restricted but not immobilized, following new guidelines for out-of-hospital trauma care. (*Source: R. Bryan Simon.*)

ESSENTIALS

DEEP WATER SOLOING
SAFETY STEPS FOR A FUN NEW SPORT

By R. Bryan Simon and Seth C. Hawkins

In deep water soloing (DWS), the danger of a fall is lessened, but the potential for injury is not eliminated. At least three DWS fatalities have been reported in Europe.

POTENTIAL INJURY TYPES

Drowning. Sudden immersion in cold water raises the risk of cold shock, a syndrome characterized by uncontrolled gasping, rapid breathing, panic, and even lethal heart rhythms. For climbers in the water longer than 15 minutes, there is also a risk of cooling in peripheral tissue, which causes loss of dexterity, gross and fine motor control, and overall strength, which in turn can contribute to drowning risk.

Impact injury due to entry. These injuries are usually due to entry that is too horizontal or that is head-first. See "Fall Safety" below.

Impact injury due to submerged hazards. These range from severe bruising to fractured limbs and head and spinal injury; such impacts also increase drowning risk due to entrapment or unconsciousness underwater.

FALL SAFETY

- Know how to swim!
- Don't go solo. Watch each other's landings and be prepared to assist if needed. If a climber is unconscious, you have only a few minutes for rescue.
- Consider the height. The higher you climb, the harder you fall and the greater the associated risk of injury.
- Practice safe entry. The regular entry is feet together, body loose, head upright, and arms tight to body. For short falls, the armchair (arms outstretched and knees bent) limits depth of entry.
- Do not look down. Doing so will cause the body to tip forward and increases the risk of head injury upon entry.

LANDING ZONES

Always check the depth of the landing zone. This can fluctuate due to tide, lake levels, and rough seas. Check for submerged rocks or flotsam such as trees.

Calm water (such as an inland lakes) has greater surface tension and will make for a harder impact. Rough or interrupted water, while making for a softer landing, may make it difficult to exit the water.

Identify exit locations prior to climbing. Consider placing fixed exit ropes to assist egress, placing spotters with throw bags at key points for rescue, or having a boat available for rescues or rest time.

R. Bryan Simon, RN, and Seth C. Hawkins, MD, are co-authors of Vertical Aid: Essential Wilderness Medicine for Climbers, Trekkers, and Mountaineers.

WYOMING

STRANDED | Inexperience, Off Route
Grand Teton, Exum Ridge

Climber 1 (24-year-old male) and Climber 2 (27-year-old female) each had been climbing for about two years. They had limited alpine experience, and this was their first climb together. On July 3 they went to Jenny Lake Ranger Station for information. Their initial plan had been to climb the North Ridge of the Grand Teton, but after talking to rangers in the station they decided to attempt the complete Exum Ridge in a day.

The two left Lupine Meadows trailhead the next morning at 2 a.m. and were starting the Lower Exum Ridge at 8 a.m. After two pitches they felt like they were moving slower than expected but decided to continue. Late in the day, they were confused about their location; they were unaware that they had completed the last pitch of the Lower Exum and continued up past Wall Street on the upper ridge. (The color of the rock was dark, and they thought they were still on the Black Face, near the top of the Lower Exum.) At dusk they were off route and doing difficult climbing above the Wind Tunnel of the Upper Exum. They rappelled back down to the top of the Golden Staircase (just above Wallstreet) in the dark and made the call for assistance.

At 10:30 p.m. rangers received a report of two climbers who were uninjured but stuck, cold, and lost. They reported their location as the Lower Exum Ridge. Rangers Harder and Hardesty were stationed at the Lower Saddle and made multiple attempts to locate the headlamps of the stranded climbers. At 1 a.m., having failed to locate their position, rangers advised the distressed climbers to stay where they were and not attempt to rappel in the dark.

At 4:58 a.m., Harder and Hardesty saw the headlamps of the climbers on the Upper Exum Ridge and confirmed contact with multiple light flashes. Harder and Hardesty, along with one bystander and two Exum guides, traveled to the top of the Golden Staircase and reached the stranded climbers at 7:45 a.m., then assisted them back to the Lower Saddle. (*Source: National Park Service Search and Rescue Report.*)

ANALYSIS
Route-finding often is difficult in the Tetons, where complex terrain and face climbing along indistinct features is the norm. With more experience on alpine rock, especially within a given mountain range, climbers develop a better sense of how to follow a route description. These climbers would have been better off choosing a shorter route for their first climb together in the Tetons. This incident also reinforces the importance of carrying adequate clothing, food, water, and possibly emergency shelter for an unexpected night out. (*Source: The Editors.*)

RAPPEL ERROR | Water Knot in Anchor Tether Came Untied
Grand Teton, Owen-Spalding Rappel

On July 23, at about 10:30 a.m., an individual high on the Grand Teton reported by cell phone that he had heard a person fall from above, hit a ledge near him, and then continue down into Valhalla Canyon near the Black Ice Couloir. Shortly thereafter, ranger Bellino received an additional call informing him that a working guide had fallen unroped from the top of the Owen-Spalding rappel. A ranger on the scene was unable to locate the fallen climber at or near the Upper Saddle. A helicopter conducted a reconnaissance flight, and at about 11:55 a.m. a body was spotted approximately 2,500 feet down Valhalla Canyon from the rappel site.

A subsequent investigation determined that the victim was a 42-year-old professional guide. He had led three students and their chaperone to the summit of the Grand via the Owen-Spalding Route. During the descent, he fell from the stance at the top of the standard Owen-Spalding rappel.

ANALYSIS

When he fell, the guide was trying to free a rappel device that was attached to the end of a belay rope and was stuck in a crack about 40 feet below him. (He is believed to have been hauling the device back to the stance after one client used it for a belayed rappel to the Upper Saddle.) Although several witnesses initially said that the guide had unclipped his lanyard from the anchor, the fall was likely due to the failure of a knot on his lanyard.

Numerous witnesses stated that the guide was secured to the anchor prior to the fall. Several of the witnesses noted that he was, at times, weighting the lanyard. After the fall, a 98-inch section of blue 9/16-inch tubular webbing was found entwined in his harness. An overhand knot was

The Grand Teton from Valhalla Canyon, showing the long fall suffered by a mountain guide when his anchor tether failed at the top of the Owen-Spalding rappel. *NPS Photo*

found in one end of the webbing. A photo taken prior to the technical portion of the climb shows that this webbing was tied in a loop with a water knot. One tail is visible and is of adequate length, but the knot is not tightened.

According to other guides familiar with the techniques used on the route, the guide may not have used this 9/16-inch webbing until he arrived at the Owen-Spalding rappel, meaning he would not have weighted the knot until that point in the day. The guide likely would have repeatedly weighted and unweighted the lanyard during the process of belaying his first client down the rappel, pulling up the belay rope, and then trying to free the stuck rappel device. Several studies have focused on the tendency of water knots to slip and fail when the tails are of inadequate length and when the knots are cyclically loaded and unloaded. One of these studies highlights the tendency for a significant amount of tail slippage to occur during initial loading, which would have been the case had the guide not weighted the lanyard until that point in the day.

All the evidence leads to the conclusion that the guide was tethered to the anchor with webbing that was tied in a loop with a water knot, that one of the tails

A 9/16-inch sling with an overhand knot, found with the climbing guide who fell from the Owen-Spalding rappel on the Grand Teton. Investigators concluded this sling, used to tether the guide at the rappel anchor, had been tied with a water knot that came undone under load. *NPS Photo*

on the knot was of inadequate length, that the tail slipped through the knot, causing it to fail while he was weighting the lanyard, and that this caused him to fall from the rappel stance. (*Source: National Park Service Search and Rescue Report.*)

EDITOR'S NOTE: *A water knot should be tied with both tails protruding from the knot at least three inches, and the knot must be retightened periodically. This tragic death of a professional guide reminds us that all climbers, even the most experienced among us, must adhere to the same fundamentals of climbing, including regularly inspecting knots and equipment.*

FAILURE TO SELF-ARREST
Grand Teton National Park, Middle Teton

At approximately 1:18 p.m. on July 24, Teton Interagency Dispatch Center received a call from a group of 20 hikers that had summited the Middle Teton and were descending the South Fork of Garnet Canyon. The caller reported that a 25-year-old female member of their group had fallen on snow, slid into rocks, cut her head, and punctured her right hip. The patient had an ice axe but was unable to self-arrest. She had a climbing helmet but was not wearing it at the time of the fall.

A helicopter reconnaissance located the patient, near the granite slabs at the top of the Cave Couloir, and ranger Tyson and Teton helitack Stull were delivered to an unimproved landing zone approximately 100 meters away. Tyson and Stull administered first aid to the patient and recommended a short-haul evacuation. Tyson and the patient were short-hauled by helicopter 38HX to Lupine Meadows. (*Source: National Park Service Search and Rescue Report.*)

ANALYSIS
Nearly every year, climbers and mountain hikers are injured in falls on hard snow in Garnet Canyon. Practice self-arrest and do not attempt to descend steep snowfields unless you are certain the snow is soft enough to travel safely. Keep your helmet on until you reach the trail, as protection against tumbling falls on snow and in talus. You have to carry it anyway—why not carry it on your head? (*Source: The Editors.*)

LEADER FALL AND LOST GEAR LEAD TO STRANDING
Grand Teton, Petzoldt Ridge

On August 9, at approximately 4:15 p.m., ranger Schuster received a transferred cell phone call from a climbing party on the Lower Exum Ridge of the Grand Teton. The caller stated that he was in visual and voice contact with two climbers on the Petzoldt Ridge, one of whom had taken a 25-foot fall but was not injured. The Petzoldt climbers indicated they had lost their climbing rack and did not have the ability to rappel off the ridge or climb any more technical rock.

At 5:55 p.m., helicopter 38HX with pilot Wilson and rangers Bellino and Armitage departed Lupine Meadows Rescue Cache and performed a reconnaissance flight. Ranger Armitage was successfully inserted to the stranded climbers' location. He prepared the climbers for a short-haul extraction, and the pair was flown directly to Lupine Meadows, arriving at 7:15 p.m.

ANALYSIS

The stranded climbers, both age 20, were interviewed at the Rescue Cache. Climber 1 had approximately four years of alpine climbing experience, including climbs in Alaska, Peru, and the Alps. However, he did not have any significant alpine rock experience; he stated that he had completed traditional rock climbs up to 5.9. Climber 2 only had 1.5 years of experience that was limited to gym and sport routes. They were carrying a single 60-meter rope, four camming devices, one set of nuts, four hexes, and eight runners. Neither had climbed in the Teton Range before.

The rescued climbers had departed their camp at the Moraine at 3:45 a.m. and were at the base of the route at 6 a.m. They reached the base of the "Window Pitch," about halfway up the route, around noon. Here, they had trouble with route-finding and spent the next four hours trying to determine the correct line. By this point both climbers were exhausted and were experiencing symptoms of extreme dehydration and fatigue, including cramping in their fingers and lightheadedness. Attempting the next pitch, Climber 1 took a 25-foot leader fall, which did not injure him but separated him from all of his wired nuts, equating to half of the team's rock protection. Climber 2 lowered him to a large ledge on the north side of the Petzoldt Ridge, and the two yelled for help.

The climbers acknowledged they had severely underestimated the physical strength and endurance required by the route. It is important to choose routes that are well within your ability, especially in a location that is unfamiliar. These climbers also packed a fairly light rack for this climb, giving them few options in case of lost gear or the need to retreat. (*Sources: National Park Service Search and Rescue Report and the Editors.*)

STRANDED | Cited for Creating Hazard
Mt. Moran, Falling Ice Glacier

On August 11, at approximately 4 p.m., a woman went to the Lupine Meadows Rescue Cache to report that her friend, a 30-year-old male, was stuck on Mt. Moran and needed help. They had had been communicating by two-way family radio. With the use of the radio, it was confirmed that he was on the Falling Ice Glacier on Mt. Moran and unable to descend.

Based on the stranded climber's location, lateness of the day, availability of the park contract helicopter, and the fact that a ground-based rescue would put rangers into an area known to have considerable rockfall and icefall hazard, it was determined that a helicopter evacuation would be the safest form of rescue. At

5:45 p.m., helicopter 38HX left Lupine Meadows with rangers Bellino and Jernigan aboard. The helicopter landed directly on the glacier, near the stranded climber's location, and the rangers helped the climber onboard the aircraft along with his pack for the flight back to Lupine Meadows.

ANALYSIS

Rangers interviewed the rescued individual in an effort to find out why he was in a position to need a rescue. He stated that he had acquired his information

about climbing Mt. Moran from Summit Post, an online mountaineering resource. He did not consult any of the local publications nor stop at the Jenny Lake Ranger Station to acquire current route information. He was equipped with mountaineering boots, ice axe, crampons, harness, belay device, five meters of small-diameter rope, several carabiners, and camping equipment. He left the Leigh Lake Trailhead around 6 a.m. on Tuesday morning, August 10, hiked around the south shore of Leigh Lake, and bush-

A climber rappels the CMC Route on Mt. Moran, with the Falling Ice Glacier in the background. *Bradly J. Boner / www. bradlyjboner.com*

whacked toward the mouth of Leigh Canyon and then up the Falling Ice drainage to the base of the glacier. Here, he decided to follow rock on the right (north) side of the glacier and avoid the main ice face. Once on the top of the glacier, he set up camp. He did not have a backcountry permit for camping.

Early Wednesday morning, the climber ascended a 300-foot, near-vertical rock face with much loose rock toward the notch between the CMC Route and the Drizzlepuss gendarme. Partway through this ascent, he decided the route he had chosen was too difficult and hazardous, so he climbed back down to the glacier. Unable to find a way to continue his descent off the glacier, he called his friend via radio for help.

Other than conveying that he was attempting to climb Mt. Moran, the individual was unable to provide the name of any known route that he was attempting. Other than the CMC route, none of the climbs on Moran that are described on Summit Post ascend anywhere near the Falling Ice Glacier, and the description of the CMC Route does not advocate climbing anywhere near the area this person was located. Had he talked to the Jenny Lake ranger staff, they would have strongly discouraged him from solo climbing Mt. Moran via the Falling Ice Glacier. With one ice axe, crampons, and boots, the rescued individual was equipped to climb steep snow, but he did not have a partner nor any rock climbing protection, making the rope he carried completely useless for fall protection. With only five meters of rope, it also was nearly useless for descending, even if he had found an adequate anchor to rappel from.

The Falling Ice Glacier is situated in a narrow hanging canyon, and there is little margin for error when entering this area via helicopter. The landing zone is crevassed and located in the rockfall zone of the Black Rock face of Mt. Moran. Based on this climber's inadequate preparation, equipment, skills, and self-reliance, as well as a disregard for others' well-being, the rescued individual received a citation for disorderly conduct—creating or maintaining a hazardous condition. (*Source: National Park Service Search and Rescue Report.*)

EDITOR'S NOTE: *Rangers in Grand Teton National Park, as with most other SAR teams in the United States, do not bill people for the cost of the rescues they perform. However, Grand Teton and other jurisdictions occasionally have issued citations when they feel a climber's egregious lack of preparation has created a hazardous situation for rescuers or others.*

PENDULUM FALL | Off Route, Inadequate Protection
Grand Teton National Park, Nez Perce

On August 22, a 36-year-old female climber and her climbing partner left the Lupine Meadows Trailhead, headed for the south ridge of Nez Perce (III 5.7). The climber's partner planned to lead the entire route. Around the seventh pitch, the leader got off route. In this area, the standard route makes a long traverse onto the east face of Nez Perce, avoiding a steep step that is home to the Garnet Traverse Variation (III 5.8). The leader reportedly began up the Garnet Traverse face before making a traverse back toward the east face. He was unable to protect this traverse. When the second climber arrived at this traverse, she broke a foothold and took a large, swinging fall to the right, using her feet and legs to protect her body from colliding with the rock.

The patient removed her climbing shoe from her right foot immediately after the fall and saw that three of her toes were black and blue. She was unable to replace the climbing shoe. She and her partner decided the easiest way off the mountain would be to continue up to the top and down the normal descent. The patient's partner continued leading, and the patient completed the remainder of the route in her approach shoes, experiencing significant pain. She and her partner then began descending the Northwest Couloir toward the South Fork of Garnet Canyon. She had to crawl, butt scoot, and crab walk to make slow progress downward. After getting off route several times, they decided to bivy at 11:30 p.m., at the top of the long talus slope leading into the South Fork.

At around 8:15 a.m. the patient reached Teton Interagency Dispatch Center by phone and reported they were still about 500 feet higher than the South Fork. She could not assess whether she had good distal circulation, sensation, and motion, due to the pain and the cold night out. The caller said she would continue moving down and estimated it would take her one to two hours to reach the floor of the South Fork. She was asked to try to find a spot where she thought a helicopter might be able to land.

Rangers Armitage and Edmonds flew into the South Fork of Garnet Canyon but were unable to locate the patient from the air. They landed and questioned other visitors, who advised them that the patient and her partner were down the canyon.

The rangers hiked down to the patient's location, arriving at about 10:30 a.m. The rangers splinted the patient's foot and assisted her in hiking back up to the landing zone, from which she was flown to Lupine Meadows. Ranger Edmonds and the partner hiked to the trailhead together. (*Source: National Park Service Search and Rescue Report.*)

Nez Perce (11,901 feet) in the Tetons. The south ridge is prominent in center left. *Acroterion, Wikimedia Commons*

ANALYSIS

Rock climbs in the Tetons are notoriously difficult to follow from route descriptions and topos. The patient had spoken by phone with a ranger at the Jenny Lake Ranger Station several times during the day prior to the climb. An in-person visit might have been more helpful, as the rangers often can point out key sections of routes in photographs.

The direct south ridge of Nez Perce has quite a long approach and descent and about 1,000 feet of technical climbing, making it a challenge to do in a day. This party's 7 a.m. start was late for such a significant outing. The fact that it was already evening at the time of the accident suggests the leader may have been feeling time pressure, possibly contributing to getting off route and failing to protect the traverse for the second. A predawn start would have given them more time to find the correct route and to get off the mountain once the patient was injured. (*Source: The Editors.*)

FALL ON ROCK | Fatigue, Inadequate Protection
Wind River Range, Warbonnet Peak

Birch Malotky and I met in Colorado and spontaneously made plans to travel the next day to the Wind River Range to climb in the Cirque of the Towers. Our goal was Black Elk on Warbonnet Peak, which has a 5.11 offwidth crux on pitch four. We began the climb late on the morning of August 24 and moved somewhat slowly. I took the crux pitch and felt very tired in the offwidth. After bumping my two number 4 Camalots up the crack, I decided to run it out to the anchor. My left foot slipped and the resulting fall was quite big because I had told Birch to give me a lot of slack so a fall wouldn't slam me over the prominent roof on the pitch. During the fall, as my arms slid down inside the crack, the pinkie finger of my right hand got stuck between a cam and the rock, and my finger was lacerated severely.

Birch lowered me to the anchor and we then made four rappels, returned to base camp, packed up camp, and hiked out. We drove to the hospital in Lander to get the finger cleaned, X-rayed, and stitched. Some tendons were damaged but not cut, and the X-ray exam found metal fragments inside the finger, probably from the anodized finish of a brand-new Camalot. The finger would recover, but it was expected to take three months before I could fully climb again.

ANALYSIS

We started the wall too late, tired from the long drive and hike in the day before, and it was the first time we had done a multi-pitch or trad climb as a team. I had the opportunity to borrow a third big cam from friends below the route, but I declined. I'd been climbing for 16 years and am a professional climber in my native Ecuador, and I didn't think the route would be a big problem. Some of my learnings from this incident are to climb for yourself and don't try to show off. On any big climb it's important to be rested, hydrate well, and communicate as a team about your energy levels, timing, and objectives. (*Source: Felipe Proaño. An interview with this climber was featured in "Ego Dangers," Episode 9 of the Sharp End podcast.*)

FIFTY-FOOT LEDGE FALL | Climbing Unroped
Wind Rivers, Cirque of the Towers, Sharks Nose

On the morning of August 26, I launched from the Big Sandy Trailhead to attempt a Cirque of the Towers traverse in a day. (*This route links eight peaks with 5.6 to 5.8 climbing and extensive scrambling and hiking.*) I had completed the traverse in one day, car to car, in 2013, and I was familiar with all portions of the route.

At the base of Sharks Nose, about midway through the traverse, I paused to eat and noted that the weather was colder and windier than forecast. I assessed my energy/mojo level at an honest 90 percent. I figured it would be easier to bail, if needed, past the traverse's technical portion. Two technical towers remained.

I forged up the Thoroughfare route on the northwest face of Sharks Nose to the notch between the south and north summits. I had brought gear for the route's rappels and to rope-solo the 5.8 crux mantel on Sharks Nose if conditions warranted, but I elected to free solo, having "floated it" twice before. However, I was unable to complete the move, nor step back down to the spire that I had just stepped off. I held a "beached whale" position for less than a minute and then fell. I latched a very sloping ledge about 15 feet below, but I was unable to hold on and again started free-falling. I landed on a three-foot ledge about 50 feet below. I was pretty intact and never lost consciousness. I shook off the daze and got to work on self-rescue, since my injuries seemed minimal. I declined help from some climbers on the ground (about 500 feet below) who had seen me fall.

I used my 66-meter rope to rappel Sharks Nose's east face, using cordage and gear I had brought or found, as there were no fixed anchors. When I arrived back at the base, my injured knee wouldn't bend enough for my foot to get back into my right running shoe. The party who had offered to help before had waited during my descent, and now I asked for their assistance. It had been about two hours since my fall.

The climbers had an inReach device in camp one mile away, and one of them set out to retrieve it while the other helped me through the talus. Soon, approximately a dozen climbers in the area were assisting with my rescue, including a physician.

My hopes for making this recue non-technical were dashed as the afternoon

Helicopter and rescuers in the Cirque of the Towers. *Tip Top Search and Rescue*

turned to evening and I learned that a helicopter was on the way. [*Tip Top Search and Rescue (TTSAR) was notified by officials in Fremont County at 4:35 p.m. that a rescue had been requested. Fremont County dispatched a helicopter with an emergency medical services crew.*] The helicopter medics arrived with a backboard, but progress was slow. Inefficiencies were introduced with a dozen or so helpers and were compounded by the lack of a clear leader. Ropes were being used in third-class terrain, and gridlock developed. Eventually, a request was made for a second helicopter with short-haul capability. [TTSAR *flew into the Cirque on a short-haul-capable helicopter. After waiting for winds to calm, near darkness, the patient was short-hauled to a landing zone east of Lonesome Lake and transferred to the other helicopter, whose crew, equipped with night-vision goggles, was able to fly out that night to Lander Regional Hospital. The other helicopter had to remain in the Cirque overnight.*]

My injuries included a broken right patella, three knocked-out teeth, five facial fractures, a broken nose, a laceration on my left patella needing 10 stitches, and road rash. Not bad for a 50-foot ledge fall!

ANALYSIS

Though I am used to long days soloing in the mountains, I consciously continued on a large objective even when my self-assessment indicated a (relatively) low level of energy. Overconfidence in the form of "I've done this before, I can just blast it out again" overwhelmed me and ended up requiring a non-trivial rescue that put rescuers at risk. I regret the helicopter noise in the Cirque that day and the next morning; it ruined the magic that the Cirque holds, which most of us appreciate and travel long distances to know. (*Source: Dave Kesonie.*)

EDITOR'S NOTE: *The climber, age 39, has been climbing for 24 years, making frequent solo trips in the Tetons and Wind Rivers. The equipment he carried and his ability to self-rescue made a fundamental difference in his outcome. It is worth noting that once outside assistance is requested, one never knows exactly what direction a rescue will take, given the variables of available resources and personnel, including their experience level and climbing ability. As climbers, it is also worth considering the potential cascade of consequences of a rescue—specifically, in this case, the grounding of a helicopter and crew members for a night in the backcountry. (Sources: Dave Kesonie, Tip Top Search and Rescue, and the Editors.)*

RAPPEL ERROR | No Backup
Devils Tower

As she prepared to rappel the Durrance Route's approach pitch, an experienced, 56-year-old climber decided to partially coil the ropes and carry them with her as she descended, so she could avoid knocking rocks on people below. During her rappel, the coils became tangled. She stopped at a small stance to untangle the coils, and when she leaned back to resume rappelling, she "somersaulted" about 20 feet down the face with the ropes moving freely through her rappel device. She came to a stop about 30 feet above the ground when the ropes tangled again and stopped running through her device. The climber's ankle was fractured in the fall. She was able to resume rappelling and reach the ground with a fireman's belay from people at the base, and after first aid she was packaged in a litter and carried to the road to meet an ambulance.

ANALYSIS
It appears likely that when the patient stopped to untangle the ropes, she accidentally grabbed either the wrong strands of rope or a single strand with her brake hand. When she weighted the ropes again, she fell. An autoblock or other third-hand backup likely would have prevented this fall.

Carrying coils of rope while rappelling can be a good choice at a place like Devils Tower, where the many cracks can snag ropes, wind may blow the ropes far to one side, or, in a case like this, for the safety of others below. It can also be a useful technique with small-diameter ropes that tangle easily. The techniques for stacking and carrying coils so they feed out slack easily during the rappel must be learned and practiced. Seek good instruction. (*Source: Lucas Barth, seasonal climbing ranger, and the Editors.*)

LEADER FALL | Inadequate Protection for Wide Crack
Vedauwoo, Nautilus

A climber with less than three years of experience attempted Mother I (5.7+ wide crack) with limited appropriately sized protection, which required bumping pieces up the crack as he ascended. The climber placed cams at 10 feet, 45 feet, and 60 feet, and he was in the process of moving up the highest cam (above him at the time) when his feet slipped out of the offwidth crack. As the leader was falling, the belayer was able to take in a bit of slack. The climber's fall was arrested when he was about five feet from the ground. He had minor lacerations and extensive abrasions from Vedauwoo's rough granite, but, amazingly, no worse injuries.

ANALYSIS
Climbs of this style often feel very difficult for their grade, especially to climbers still mastering wide crack techniques. During one's apprenticeship, it's important to carry plenty of protection. Making use of a limited rack by bumping pieces up the crack (moving them with you as you climb) is an effective tactic, but it leaves the climber vulnerable to a very long fall in case of a mistake. One technique is to clip the piece you're bumping to the rope with a long runner—you won't have to pull up as much heavy rope and/or reclip the piece each time you move it up the crack.

Although this climber did not hit his head in his long fall, he noted that he should have worn a helmet. (*Sources: Anonymous report and the Editors.*)

Mt. Tupper's summit pyramid, with the upper west ridge at left. *Parks Canada*

CANADA

Unless otherwise noted, reports in the Canada section were drawn from national and regional park summaries. The analyses were provided by park rangers or Robert Chisnall of the Alpine Club of Canada.

FATAL FALL | Loose Rock, Climbing Unroped
British Columbia, Glacier National Park, Mt. Tupper

On July 25, while ascending the classic west ridge of Mt. Tupper, an unroped climber pulled on a loose block along the ridge top and fell down the south face. His two climbing partners witnessed him falling with the large block, then cartwheeling out of sight. They immediately called for help and a helicopter reconnaissance located the fallen climber approximately 200 meters below the ridge, showing signs of major trauma. A decision was made to extricate the two climbing partners before recovering the body. This would reduce the possibility of rockfall hitting rescuers, and it would remove the traumatized climbers from the scene. Both the climbers and, eventually, the victim were heli-slung from the mountain.

ANALYSIS
When climbing mountain routes, there will always be sections of loose rock. It is recommended to slow down, put on a rope, and belay through loose sections, if possible. The nature of this particular route lends itself well to short-roping and short-pitching–two techniques that allow mountaineers to move efficiently through terrain while protected by a rope and their partner.

STRANDED | Inadequate Equipment
British Columbia, Glacier National Park, Mt. Tupper

On June 20, as a pair of climbers was ascending the south buttress of Mt. Tupper, wet, snowy conditions slowed their progress in the upper third of the route. The climbers did not bring ice axes and crampons for traversing the final snowy ledges to the west ridge near the top, nor did they carry bivouac gear. The pair realized they were a long ways from the top and that they were unprepared to retreat or continue. They stopped on a sloping, three-meter-wide ledge and called Jasper dispatch for a rescue. A Parks Canada Visitor Safety team responded via helicopter, and both climbers were slung out.

ANALYSIS

As mountaineering routes dry off at the beginning of the climbing season, one needs to remember there may still be lots of snow lingering on ledges. The previous week had brought much rainfall, so there was a lot of moisture running down the mountain. The quartzite on Mt. Tupper is generally quite solid, but much of it is covered with a thin veneer of lichen that becomes very slippery when wet. Had the climbing party taken more time to scope their intended route, they would have seen dark water streaks in most of the corners, indicating the route was not dry. They also did not bring the appropriate gear to complete the route (ice axe and crampons).

SCRAMBLING FALL | Loose Hold
British Columbia, Glacier National Park, Sulzer Tower

At the end of August, a party of three climbers attempted a lightweight traverse of the peaks that bound the headwaters of the Illecillewaet River, including Mt. Sir Donald. This is a 37-kilometer trip with nearly 6,000 meters of vertical gain and loss. The group was traveling extremely light, with just the bare necessities for their objective.

After successfully summiting Avalanche Mountain and Eagle Peak, the group was scrambling up Sulzer Tower en route to Uto Peak. The climber in the back inadvertently pulled on a loose block while navigating a steep step and fell 35 to 40 meters to a scree ledge, sustaining severe injuries. His climbing partners descended to him and provided initial first aid, but recognized they would need a rescue as soon as possible. With unreliable cell coverage at the injury site, one member reascended their route toward the summit of Eagle Peak and was able to call for help.

A Parks Canada field crew was in a helicopter immediately across the valley when the call came in. They diverted from their course and were able to locate the injured climber within 10 minutes of the call. A second helicopter with a rescue pilot was called in, and the Parks Canada team long-lined into the crash site, packaged the patient, and had the patient down to the highway within two hours of the initial call. The patient was transferred to BC Air Ambulance immediately. He had a broken pelvis, broken back, and multiple open wounds to his face, back, and arms.

ANALYSIS

The peaks near Rogers Pass have some very solid quartzite, but as with all mountains, there are loose sections to be negotiated. Care must be taken to avoid loose rock as best you can, pulling down instead of out on holds, and slowing down when you are among chossy blocks. This group was very experienced, but one pull on a loose block resulted in one of them taking a very long fall that easily could have been fatal. The victim's helmet was smashed in multiple spots, and he likely would have suffered a traumatic head injury if it weren't for the helmet. The team did well to stabilize the patient and call for help.

BOULDER CRUSHES BUGABOOS CLIMBER: On July 15, a loose boulder shifted as a 32-year-old apprentice guide approached the west ridge of Pigeon Spire, sending him into a 10-meter tumble. The boulder then rolled over the climber, breaking 14 ribs and two vertebrae and collapsing a lung; his helmet was crushed in the fall but he did not have a head injury. He was rescued by helicopter later the same day. We did not receive a firsthand report on this incident, but it is included in our data.

LONG LEADER FALL ON ICE | Inadequate Protection
British Columbia, Yoho National Park, Carlsberg Column

On December 28, two experienced climbers started up the classic Field ice climb known as Carlsberg Column. Carlsberg has an "approach pitch" that starts out with a steep little pillar (WI3) and then continues for another 30 meters of low-angled ice to reach a large ledge below the main route. After climbing the steep part of the approach pitch with no protection, the leader placed an ice screw and continued up the easier terrain, placing one more screw in good ice. Somewhere near the end

of the pitch, he was preparing to place another screw when he fell, sliding down the low-angled ice and then flying over the steep section before his partner caught the fall, stopping him 10 meters above the ground. The total fall distance was estimated at 25 meters.

During the long fall, the leader slammed his feet into the ice and broke both of his ankles. When he came to a stop, he was conscious and a quick inventory revealed no other injuries except for the ankles. His partner lowered him to the ground and proceeded to make him comfortable before calling 911 for a rescue. Ultimately, the climber was evacuated to a waiting ambulance using a helicopter sling-rescue system.

ANALYSIS

While it is tempting to climb long distances between protection pieces when the climbing is not difficult, this tactic significantly increases the risk of an injurious leader fall. Anyone can fall while ice climbing—it doesn't matter how good you are or how long you have been climbing. In this case, the climber had done the climb repeatedly and at times had soloed the approach pitch. The climber

Diagram of the fall on Carlsberg Column's first pitch. *Parks Canada*

believes a tool placement that had appeared solid actually had fractured the ice significantly, and when he went to place his other tool the first tool popped out. When placing protection requires little effort, take the extra moment to place a few more ice screws, even when you don't think you will fall. *Editor's note: An interview with this climber was featured in Episode 13 of the Sharp End podcast. Search "Two Screws, Two Ankles."*

FATAL FALL | Loose Rock, Climbing Unroped
British Columbia, Mt. Assiniboine, North Ridge

A party of two departed the Hind Hut at 5:30 a.m. on August 30 to attempt the north ridge of Mt. Assiniboine. This is the most popular route up this peak, rated 5.5 and Alpine Grade II. Moving relatively quickly, the two climbers gained the ridge at first light. The previous day, they had discussed transitioning to roped climbing at the first steep section, called the Red Band. When the first climber arrived at the Red Band, however, he proceeded to solo this section. When his partner arrived they discussed the change from their original plan, but the first climber was reluctant to downclimb, so after finding an easier route to the right, the second climber soloed the Red Band as well.

After the Red Band, the terrain eased off and the two moved together, still unroped, a few meters apart. Approximately 100 meters below the second steep section, called the Grey Band, the second climber communicated to his partner that it was "time to put the rope on." After a brief discussion and another 50 meters of exposed climbing, the first climber finally agreed that the terrain was too hazardous to continue without a rope. They decided to move up to a small perch that would provide a suitable spot to rope up.

As the first climber moved toward the ledge, his left handhold broke free and he began to fall. The second climber watched him tumble down the north face until he was out of sight. The second climber triggered his SPOT device and then slowly downclimbed to lower-angle terrain and waited for help to arrive. Another climbing party arrived and began to assist in the descent.

Banff dispatch received notice of the emergency SPOT activation at 10 a.m. On an initial flyover, the Parks Canada Visitor Safety team made visual contact with two other climbers on the north ridge, who pointed in the direction of the emergency. After 15 minutes of searching the north face from the helicopter, the fallen climber was located approximately 500 meters down from the site of the fall.

Mt. Assiniboine, showing the site of a fall from the north ridge on August 30. *Parks Canada*

ANALYSIS

Prior to climbing the route, the team did a good job of preparing. They studied the route and had a good understanding of the terrain they would encounter. They agreed on where they would use a rope and identified areas that they would travel unroped. They were prepared with the appropriate equipment and knowledge for a safe ascent.

Two main factors influenced the unfortunate outcome of the day:

- Early separation between the two caused a lack of communication and a departure from their original plan.
- Despite the popularity of this route and the ease of the climbing, the climb still has a lot of loose and fractured rock. This requires a great deal of care, especially when moving unroped.

It is easy to point a finger or say, "I would have never done that," but during a long climb the decision-making often is not simple. The take-home lesson is that cost/benefit decisions to determine the level of acceptable risk in the mountains must be made collaboratively. If you are going to depart from your initial plan, or if you find conditions different than expected, stop and make sure everyone in your group is on the same page before continuing.

ICE CLIMBING LEADER FALL
Banff National Park, Professor Falls

On February 21, a party was climbing Professor Falls on the slopes of Mt. Rundle and attempting to combine pitches in order to complete the route quickly. The leader, a very experienced climber in his 50s, climbed and protected the upper portion of the second pitch, walked across a low-angle ice ledge to the base of the third pitch, and started up. As he stopped to place an ice screw, he slipped and fell, slid back across the ledge, and fell down the pitch he had just climbed. He fell approximately 30 meters before being stopped by his belayer just above the belay ledge. He fractured his pelvis, vertebrae, and ankle, along with other more minor injuries.

Nearby climbing parties assisted with stabilizing the patient, while a combination of a personal locater beacon and cell phone were used to call for help. At 2:45 p.m., three Parks Canada Visitor Safety staff were slung into the scene by helicopter. The patient was packaged, slung out to a waiting ambulance, and taken to the hospital in Banff.

ANALYSIS
Why the climber fell is uncertain, but with a lot of rope out on low-angle ground, without any protection, he fell a long way. The easiest way to manage this hazard would have been to stop and belay on the sloping ledge, since protecting the low-angle ice would have resulted in a lot of rope drag for the leader on the next steep ice. The fact that he had protected the lower steep section, which allowed his belayer to stop him before the next ledge, certainly contributed to a better outcome.

This party was prepared with both a cell phone and a satellite communicator to call for help. As a result, the location and nature of the injury were quickly established, and the rescue was completed quickly. This helped prevent very serious injuries from becoming life-threatening.

SKI MOUNTAINEER HIT BY FALLING CORNICE
Alberta, Banff National Park, Mons Icefield

A group of seven skiers was attempting the southern portion of the Great Divide ski traverse, which goes from the Columbia Icefields to Lake Louise. On May 4 they were using the standard bolted rappel route off the west glacier of the Mons Icefield. This descent goes through a 100-meter rock band below a snow slope and cornice. They were on the rappels around 10 a.m. on an overcast day, following a poor freeze.

The first member of the party had just reached the ledge at the bottom of the rappels when a chunk of the cornice failed and entrained enough snow to create a size 1.5 avalanche that knocked him off the ledge and carried him about 40 meters downslope. He remained on the surface, but was sore and shaken up. The rest of the group, spread out along the four rappel stations, was unaffected. They rappelled down to reach the patient, assessed him, kept him warm, and moved him downslope away from further avalanche hazard. They called for help using an inReach device and a satellite phone.

A team of Visitor Safety specialists responded with a helicopter from Banff. Two rescuers packaged the injured skier, who was transported to the Banff hospital via helicopter. The remaining six skiers decided to abort their traverse plans and ski out to the nearest road.

ANALYSIS

This challenging traverse requires favorable avalanche conditions, weather, and snow coverage to be completed safely. The winter of 2016 was very warm and dry, and spring came early. Snowmelt in the Rockies was about one month ahead of schedule.

The Mons rappels expose you to a large cornice that overhangs the descent route and falls off every year. Cornice failures are unpredictable; however, they tend to fall

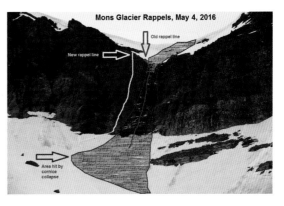

A cornice collapse covered the former rappel route (blue line) down this 100-meter rock wall. The new rappel route (yellow) was mostly untouched. *Parks Canada*

when they are big (i.e., in the spring) and when temperatures are warm or after windy periods when a lot of new cornice growth has occurred. The party chose a reasonable day with respect to the cloud cover, but the cornice would have been much more solid if they had had a good overnight freeze. They also might have avoided problems if they had done the rappels at night or earlier in the morning.

Unfortunately, on big traverses you often don't have time to wait for perfect weather conditions or timing. This team rolled the dice and lost. Fortunately for them, a few summers earlier, the Banff Visitor Safety team had moved the bolted rappel route to a more protected location in order to decrease the cornice-fall exposure. The skiers were using the new, more protected rappel line, and the six skiers who were still on the rappels when the event occurred were thus sheltered from the cornice chunks instead of being directly in the line of fire, as they would have been on the old rappel route.

EDITOR'S NOTE: *Data from several other climbing and skiing accidents in Banff National Park is included in our tables.*

LONG ICE CLIMBING FALL | Descending Unroped
Alberta, Ghost River Valley

At 3:40 p.m. on February 4, two ice climbers were descending the lower portion of the Aquarius ice climb (WI4). The first climber walked across a large ice ledge to the anchor at the top of the final rappel while his partner pulled the ropes from the previous rappel. As the first climber approached the edge, he slipped and fell approximately eight meters to the base of the route, breaking his pelvis and several vertebrae. His partner rappelled down, established the seriousness of the injuries, insulated the patient as best he could, and ran for help. A nearby group of three climbers stayed with the patient and provided additional warm clothing.

The partner hiked and drove for about an hour before finding a phone; he called for help just before dark. A joint ground response was initiated by Parks Canada, Banff EMS, and Kananaskis Country, with rescue crews reaching the injured climber at 8:45 p.m. The climber was packaged on a stretcher, lowered down the final ice steps, and transported 1.5 kilometers by wheeled stretcher to a staging area. A Shock Trauma Air Rescue Service (STARS) helicopter was able to land at the staging area, with the crew using night-vision goggles, and at 11:30 p.m. the patient was flown to a hospital in Calgary.

ANALYSIS

The initial slip occurred on relatively level ground, but the climber was not able to prevent himself from sliding over the edge. The only real preventive measure would be to stay attached to a rope or anchor while approaching an edge.

After the fall it became apparent that neither the injured party nor the nearby climbing party had any means of calling for help. This resulted in a delay of about six hours in the patient reaching the hospital. Fortunately, his injuries were not immediately life-threatening, but a satellite communication device would have resulted in a much faster helicopter rescue, during daylight hours.

Though the accident occurred on a relatively warm day, the patient was already mildly hypothermic by the time rescuers arrived; the insulation the other climbers placed between the patient and the ice allowed the patient to stay as warm as possible and certainly helped in the outcome.

LEADER FALL | Inadequate Protection
Alberta, Yamnuska, Forbidden Corner

An experienced party of two was climbing Forbidden Corner (5.9 R) on April 12 when the leader fell about 10 meters on the fourth or fifth pitch as a result of a broken hold. A piece of protection pulled out and lengthened the fall. As the belayer stopped the falling leader, the climber swung into the wall feet-first, and he sustained a compound fracture of his lower right leg. The pitch had involved traversing, and the climber ended up below and to the left of the belayer. Self-rescue would have been difficult, so the pair phoned for a rescue.

Kananaskis Public Safety responded to the call with six rescuers and a Bell 407 helicopter with slinging capabilities. A direct helicopter sling was attempted, but wind and the steep nature of the route made it too dangerous for rescue personnel. Instead, the rescue team climbed the route to access the patient. The injury was stabilized and the patient and an attending rescuer were lowered to the ground with a twin-rope rescue system.

ANALYSIS

Both climbers involved were experienced and prepared. However, the rock quality in the Canadian Rockies is less than ideal, and in this instance a hold broke with no warning, despite the climber having checked it. In the Rockies, the "three points of contact" rule is especially important: Maintaining weight distribution evenly over multiple holds allows the climber to maintain stability if one hold fails. Poor rock quality also means unreliable protection, so it's important to place pro whenever it's available, even on easier ground. (*Source: Matt Mueller, Alberta Parks, Kananaskis Public Safety.*)

ANOTHER LONG FALL ON YAMNUSKA: *On September 1, a climber broke a hold, took a 15-meter fall, and hit a ledge while leading the second or third pitch of a 5.10d route to the right of Direttissima. The fall caused a fractured hip and minor head injury. No firsthand report was available.*

LONG LEADER FALL ON ICE | Inadequate Protection
Alberta, Kananaskis Country, Waiparous Creek

On November 29, while leading the second pitch of Kemosabe (100 meters, WI4), a 35-year-old climber took a 40-meter fall from near the end of the pitch, pulling out two ice screws before his fall was arrested. The climber sustained life-threatening injuries, including a skull fracture and broken pelvis. His two climbing partners, one of whom was a doctor, stabilized him as best they could on a sloping ice ledge while awaiting a rescue. Kananaskis Country Public Safety technicians heli-slung the climber from the ledge and transported him to an air ambulance.

ANALYSIS

The injured climber was an experienced and skilled ice climber. This climb is notorious for being somewhat sandbagged and often has extensive wet or chandeliered ice on the second pitch. The climber had placed five screws before his fall–not many, considering the distance he had climbed, but he later said there was no good ice to place additional protection. Certain routes and certain conditions carry inherent risk that cannot be mitigated. As the climber acknowledged, they should not have attempted this route on that day. (*Sources: Kananaskis Country Public Safety, media reports, and the Editors.*)

SCRAMBLING FALL | Forced Bivouac
Alberta, Border Ranges, Mt. Haig

On November 13 a party of six scrambled to the summit of Mt. Haig, in the far southern Canadian Rockies, via the east ridge. At about 4 p.m., as the party was descending, one member of the group stumbled forward and at the same time lost her grip on her ice axe. This resulted in a tumbling fall of approximately 40 meters down snow-covered ledges. Details of her injuries are not available, but she was conscious and stable after the fall. With deteriorating weather and nightfall approaching, the party was able to send an SOS message from a SPOT device and text messages from a cell phone.

A team of three rescuers reached the party at 11 p.m. One rescuer stayed on scene with the injured climber through the night, using two small tents as bivy bags, while the uninjured members of the party descended with the other rescuers. The weather continued to deteriorate overnight, with wind speeds of 80–110 km/h (50–68 mph), and 10–15 cm (4–6 inches) of snowfall. The following morning, the weather improved slightly, and the injured climber and rescuer were extricated using helicopter sling rescue.

ANALYSIS

The snow patches that the route crossed were very firm due to rime ice on the surface. Each member of the group carried Microspikes, and the use of proper crampons might have prevented the fall.

Two observations can be made on this party's use of the SPOT, relevant to users of all such devices. 1) The device continued to send a location message for several hours after the initial SOS message. The group member who carried the SPOT changed locations repeatedly, which led to some confusion on the part of the rescuers. Thankfully, this climber did not move far from the injured party. 2) Once the SOS on the SPOT had been triggered, the emergency contact of the SPOT owner was notified. It would have been beneficial if this emergency contact had details of the group's trip plans.

The extra layers of clothing and emergency tarps the group carried would be sufficient for healthy people to stay warm for several hours in the weather conditions the group experienced during the day. However, with the deteriorating weather that evening, the group likely would have become hypothermic had they needed to spend the night out (especially the injured party) without assistance. They carried disposable, foil-type tarps ("space blankets"), and several of these had already been destroyed by the strong wind before the rescue party arrived.

LEADER FALL | Clipped Wrong Rope to Protection
Ontario, Metcalfe North

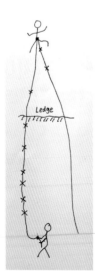

An experienced local climber, age 68, was leading Peak Season in Harlem (5.8/5.9), a nine-bolt sport route, in June. He attempted to take a rest by hanging at the ninth bolt, but when he sat back on the rope, he fell to about the height of the fourth bolt, impacting a ledge during his fall. The accident occurred around 11 a.m. His final orientation in the fall was head down. Fortunately, he was wearing a helmet.

The leader was initially unresponsive for about one minute, and he experienced a temporary loss of vision. His sight then returned and he complained about back pain. One of the climbers present called 911. Paramedics arrived at 11:33 a.m., and after an assessment and initial treatment, he was secured to a stretcher and evacuated over rugged terrain. At the hospital, it was determined that he had seven broken ribs, internal bleeding in the lower back, pulmonary edema, lacerations on his nose and arm, and low blood pressure and heart rate, which may have been related to blood-thinner medication he was taking. A lengthy but full recovery was expected.

ANALYSIS

The leader had tied into two nearly identical ropes at the front of his harness. (His intention was to trail the second rope in order to set up a top-rope on an adjacent climb, once he reached the top.) He was utilizing the newer of the two ropes as a lead rope. He correctly clipped the lead rope to the first seven bolts. However, the leader mistakenly clipped the trailing rope to the top two bolts. The belayer was unable to see the error and warn the climber. When the leader attempted to rest at the ninth bolt, he fell until the rope clipped at the seventh bolt caught his fall.

The correct method of trailing a rope is to attach it to the rear clip-in point on the harness, keeping it away from the lead rope. (*Source: Jane Howe.*)

MEXICO

CREVASSE FALL | Climbing Alone
Pico de Orizaba, Jamapa Glacier

Looking out of the Orizaba crevasse.

On the morning of February 8, Jacob "Jake" Lloyd, an experienced mountaineer from Utah, was climbing alone on the Jamapa Glacier, the normal route up the 18,491-foot mountain. At approximately 18,200 feet, a snow bridge collapsed and Jake fell about 25 feet into a crevasse. Landing on his back, he suffered only a few scrapes but was unable to climb out. Using his cell phone, Jake was able to reach an emergency number, but the message was poorly translated and responding rescuers were directed to the base of the glacier rather than his actual location. He was forced to spend a cold and sleepless night in the crevasse, warding off frostbite and cold injury by continually moving his fingers and toes.

On the morning of February 9, a Mexican guide came upon the collapsed snow bridge and located Jake. After confirming that he was uninjured, the guide continued to the summit with his clients and returned with four additional climbers. The guide and climbers lowered a rope and an additional ice axe and were able to extricate Jake from the crevasse. He was given food and water, and the climbing team escorted him down the mountain.

ANALYSIS

Climbing alone was the major contributing factor in this incident. The climber was very lucky that a guide encountered his tracks and was able to gather a team to extricate him relatively quickly. Jake also was lucky to avoid injury in his fall or frostbite during the night. The crevasse walls prevented wind chill from being much of a factor, and Jake's actions to stay awake and keep moving helped prevent a cold injury.

Though many guidebooks, trip reports, and guides state there are no large crevasses on Pico de Orizaba, climbers should always prepare for crevasses on glacial terrain, including the Jamapa Glacier. (*Sources: Scott Larson and the Editors.*)

TABLES

TABLE I: REPORTED CLIMBING ACCIDENTS

Year	Number of Accidents Reported		Total Persons Involved		Injured		Fatalities	
	USA	CAN	USA	CAN	USA	CAN	USA	CAN
1951	15	n/a	22	n/a	11	n/a	3	n/a
1952	31	n/a	35	n/a	17	n/a	13	n/a
1953	24	n/a	27	n/a	12	n/a	12	n/a
1954	31	n/a	41	n/a	31	n/a	8	n/a
1955	34	n/a	39	n/a	28	n/a	6	n/a
1956	46	n/a	72	n/a	54	n/a	13	n/a
1957	45	n/a	53	n/a	28	n/a	18	n/a
1958	32	n/a	39	n/a	23	n/a	11	n/a
1959	42	2	56	2	31	0	19	2
1960	47	4	64	12	37	8	19	4
1961	49	9	61	14	45	10	14	4
1962	71	1	90	1	64	0	19	1
1963	68	11	79	12	47	10	19	2
1964	53	11	65	16	44	10	14	3
1965	72	0	90	0	59	0	21	0
1966	67	7	80	9	52	6	16	3
1967	74	10	110	14	63	7	33	5
1968	70	13	87	19	43	12	27	5
1969	94	11	125	17	66	9	29	2
1970	129	11	174	11	88	5	15	5
1971	110	17	138	29	76	11	31	7
1972	141	29	184	42	98	17	49	13
1973	108	6	131	6	85	4	36	2
1974	96	7	177	50	75	1	26	5
1975	78	7	158	22	66	8	19	2
1976	137	16	303	31	210	9	53	6
1977	121	30	277	49	106	21	32	11
1978	118	17	221	19	85	6	42	10
1979	100	36	137	54	83	17	40	19
1980	191	29	295	85	124	26	33	8
1981	97	43	223	119	80	39	39	6
1982	140	48	305	126	120	43	24	14
1983	187	29	442	76	169	26	37	7
1984	182	26	459	63	174	15	26	6
1985	195	27	403	62	190	22	17	3

Year	Number of Accidents Reported		Total Persons Involved		Injured		Fatalities	
	USA	CAN	USA	CAN	USA	CAN	USA	CAN
1986	203	31	406	80	182	25	37	14
1987	192	25	377	79	140	23	32	9
1988	156	18	288	44	155	18	24	4
1989	141	18	272	36	124	11	17	9
1990	136	25	245	50	125	24	24	4
1991	169	20	302	66	147	11	18	6
1992	175	17	351	45	144	11	43	6
1993	132	27	274	50	121	17	21	1
1994	158	25	335	58	131	25	27	5
1995	168	24	353	50	134	18	37	7
1996	139	28	261	59	100	16	31	6
1997	158	35	323	87	148	24	31	13
1998	138	24	281	55	138	18	20	1
1999	123	29	248	69	91	20	17	10
2000	150	23	301	36	121	23	24	7
2001	150	22	276	47	138	14	16	2
2002	139	27	295	29	105	23	34	6
2003	118	29	231	32	105	22	18	6
2004	160	35	311	30	140	16	35	14
2005	111	19	176	41	85	14	34	7
2006	109	n/a	227	n/a	89	n/a	21	n/a
2007	113	n/a	211	n/a	95	n/a	15	n/a
2008	112	n/a	203	n/a	96	n/a	19	n/a
2009	126	n/a	240	n/a	112	n/a	23	n/a
2010	185	n/a	389	n/a	151	n/a	34	n/a
2011	157	n/a	348	n/a	109	n/a	29	n/a
2012	140	15	309	36	121	12	30	2
2013	143	11	283	24	100	5	21	4
2014	112	10	170	19	89	8	28	1
2015	173	20	258	52	111	16	37	4
2016	175	23	302	58	134	17	32	6
TOTAL:	7,656	1,037	14,108	2,192	6,365	773	1,662	309

TABLE II: ACCIDENTS BY LOCATION

Geographical Districts	1951–2015			2016		
	Number of Accidents	Deaths	Total Persons Involved	Number of Accidents	Deaths	Total Persons Involved
Canada*						
Alberta	555	146	1092	13	2	36
British Columbia	332	126	691	9	4	20
Yukon Territory	40	28	86	0	0	0
New Brunswick	1	0	0	0	0	0
Ontario	39	9	69	1	0	2
Québec	32	10	65	0	0	0
East Arctic	8	2	21	0	0	0
West Arctic	2	2	2	0	0	0
United States						
Alaska	610	221	1001	11	2	28
Arizona, Nevada, Texas	127	26	227	4	0	8
Atlantic–North	1155	159	1939	38	2	57
Atlantic–South	226	44	380	12	0	21
California	1520	321	885	39	13	61
Central	143	18	232	0	0	0
Colorado	959	244	2625	19	2	41
Montana, Idaho, South Dakota	100	41	159	2	0	2
Oregon	260	128	547	9	2	17
Utah, New Mex.	213	68	383	17	6	30
Washington	2039	340	1100	11	4	18
Wyoming	631	156	1170	13	1	19

*Canada figures include no data from 2006–2011; new data is included from 2012–2016

TABLE III: ACCIDENTS BY CAUSE

	1951–2015 USA	*1959–2015 CAN.	2016 USA	2016 CAN.
Terrain				
Rock	5234	563	124	15
Snow	2647	371	39	4
Ice	305	18	6	5
River	25	3	0	0
Unknown	22	11	3	0

	1951–2015 USA	*1959–2015 CAN.	2016 USA	2016 CAN.
Ascent or Descent				
Ascent	4204	615	91	16
Descent	1364	396	49	6
Unknown	282	13	26	2
Other[1]	31	2	9	0
Immediate Cause				
Fall or slip on rock	4098	307	75	9
Fall on snow or ice	1176	215	18	6
Falling rock, ice, or object	700	147	3	1
Exceeding abilities / Inexperience	603	36	1	0
Illness[2]	456	27	9	0
Stranded / Lost	404	62	14	1
Avalanche	331	130	3	3
Rappel Failure / Error[3]	398	54	16	1
Lowering Error[7]	6	0	6	1
Exposure	285	14	2	0
Loss of control / Glissade	240	18	3	0
Nut / cam pulled out	294	11	1	0
Failure to follow route	258	36	1	0
Fall into crevasse / moat	190	52	0	0
Faulty use of crampons	127	7	0	0
Piton / ice screw pulled out	95	13	0	0
Ascending too fast	75	0	4	0
Skiing[4]	70	14	3	0
Lightning	68	7	0	0
Equipment failure	18	3	0	0
Other[5]	625	39	6	0
Unknown	70	10	3	0
Contributory Causes				
Climbing unroped	1097	169	13	5
Exceeding abilities / Inexperience	1040	206	17	0
Placed no / inadequate protection	906	102	23	3
Inadequate equipment / clothing	761	73	8	1
Weather	540	76	2	0
Climbing alone	463	73	7	1
No helmet	390	75	0	0
Inadequate belay[6]	292	29	11	0
Nut / cam pulled out	233	32	11	1

	1951–2015 USA	*1959–2015 CAN.	2016 USA	2016 CAN.
Poor position	249	26	4	2
Darkness	184	22	1	1
Party separated	137	12	2	0
Failure to test holds / loose rock	123	41	8	6
Piton / ice screw pulled out	87	14	0	1
Failed to follow directions / route	89	18	9	0
Exposure	68	16	0	0
Illness[2]	41	9	0	0
Equipment failure	20	7	2	0
Other[5]	324	102	1	0
Age of Individuals				
Under 15	1249	12	0	0
15-20	1346	204	6	0
21-25	1589	259	15	0
26-30	1510	214	29	1
31-35	2156	15	9	3
36-50	3522	144	25	1
Over 50	420	35	16	2
Unknown	2263	569	59	16
Sex[7]				
Male	131	21	121	15
Female	49	4	36	3
Not known	25	0	41	5
Experience Level				
None/Little	1931	308	9	0
Moderate (1 to 3 years)	1809	359	16	0
Experienced	2476	477	53	11
Unknown	2575	594	107	12
Month				
January	272	26	6	0
February	243	58	7	2
March	384	73	14	1
April	487	41	11	1
May	1036	66	13	2
June	1268	76	23	3
July	2105	267	23	3